Charles Olson

Twayne's United States Authors Series

Warren French, Editor

University College of Swansea, Wales

TUSAS 590

CHARLES OLSON
Photograph Courtesy of Literary and Cultural Archives, University of Connecticut Libraries.

Charles Olson

Enikő Bollobás

Eötvös Coránd University, Budapest, Hungary

Twayne Publishers • New York
Maxwell Macmillan Canada • Toronto
Maxwell Macmillan International • New York Oxford Singapore Sydney

Charles Olson
Enikő Bollobás

Twayne Publishers
Macmillan Publishing Company
866 Third Avenue
New York, New York 10022

Maxwell Macmillan Canada Inc.
1200 Eglinton Avenue East
Suite 200
Don Mills, Ontario M3C 3N1

10 9 8 7 6 5 4 3 2 1

The paper used in this publication meets the minimum requirements
of American National Standard for Information Sciences—Permanence
of Paper for Printed Library Materials, ANSI Z39.48-1984. ⊗™

Printed and bound in the United States of America.

Library of Congress Cataloging-in-Publication Data

Bollobás, Enikő.
    Charles Olson / Enikő Bollobás.
        p.   cm. — (Twayne's United States authors series ; TUSAS 590)
    Includes bibliographical references and index.
    ISBN 0-8057-7629-X (alk. paper)
    1. Olson, Charles, 1910–1970—Criticism and interpretation.
I. Title.   II. Series.
PS3529.L655Z58   1992
811'.54—dc20   91-41175
                                                         CIP

For László, Gigi, and Máté: the posture, you know

Contents

Preface

I first heard about Charles Olson in 1974, when I was not yet 22. My friend and teacher, the Hungarian poet Gyula Kodolányi, gave me Olson's *Selected Writings*, to read and comment upon in class. It was one of my most difficult assignments, but my fascination with Olson's writing was instantaneous. To me, as for many of his readers, Olson became the sage, the guru, the true source of wisdom. In his poetry doors keep opening constantly, meanings are always about to arrive. Entering his mind through his poetry, the reader is given the privilege of enjoying the perpetual arrival of the "eternal events" that fill our lives.

As my fascination with Olson's ideas grew, I began to realize how much Olson resembled my own father. Although father's field was human medicine, he oftentimes said things that sounded like Olson, whose fatherly guidelines for Ed Dorn in "A Bibliography on America for Ed Dorn" are much like the advice I grew up with: "Best thing to do is *to dig one thing or place or man* until you yourself know more abt that than is possible to any other man. It doesn't matter whether it's Barbed Wire or Pemmican or Paterson or Iowa. But *exhaust* it. Saturate it. Beat it. And then U KNOW everything else very fast: one saturation job (it might take 14 years). And you're in, forever."[1]

So Charles Olson became part of my life. His sentences resonated in my head, became indistinguishable from the words of my father—and also from those of my fatherly old friend, Rabbi Scheiber, the world-renowned scholar of Judaism. Their *posture* made them inhabit the same world of passion and knowledge. They lived according to a strict hierarchy of values, based upon ideas of dignity and humility, ideas seated behind their anthropologically similar-looking heads and foreheads. (How could this be true for a Swedish-American, a Jewish Hungarian, and a very mixed Hungarian?) They all left this world in a very similar way: all three died of cancer of the liver (live-her, as Olson would say).

Charles Olson is, I am quite sure, one of the most difficult poets to write a book about, especially a book intended for students. I begin, for this reason, as far back as possible, with Olson's personal and historical background. To understand Olson the poet, one must be familiar with

Olson the person—this truly unusual man, teacher, and preacher, of vast body size and even larger spirit. His towering figure has to be put into perspective, into the intellectual space populated by such companions as Herman Melville, Corrado Cagli, Edward Dahlberg, Carl Sauer, Ezra Pound, Franklin Roosevelt, D. H. Lawrence, and William Carlos Williams, as well as his friends and students at Black Mountain College, where he found his true communal city.

Chapter 2 offers a reading of Olson's best-known essays, "Projective Verse" and "Human Universe." Chapter 3 examines Olson's epistemology and his creative use of language. Chapter 4 focuses on Olson's poetry exclusive of *The Maximus Poems*. Although I offer a general appraisal of each volume that came out in Olson's lifetime, I devote the most attention to such major pieces as "The Kingfishers," "The Praises," "In Cold Hell, in Thicket," and "Variations Done for Gerald Van De Wiele." Chapter 5 offers an overview of Olson's greatest achievement, *The Maximus Poems*. After discussing the work's overall structure, I examine some individual pieces—those that serve, I think, as representation of the whole long poem in terms of theme, method, and range of interests. This book does not attempt to analyze the full Olson oeuvre; such a task would be impossible to accomplish within the format of the series. My book is intended as an introduction and guide; I hope that it will help to usher the interested reader into further studies.

I want to thank my dead fathers for creating the interest, the attention, and the affinity, without which no book could have been born. For their scholarly support and guidance I am indebted to Gyula Kodolányi and to Warren French, who read the manuscript with care and concern, and made comments that contributed to its improvement. The class of English 410 of spring quarter 1987 at the University of Oregon (Eugene) provided inspiration and enthusiasm; I especially owe thanks to Rob Halpern, Eve Mills, Jim Cartwright, Rebecca Weeks and Brad Allen. And to my immediate family—László, Gigi, Máté, and Nelly—who shared the work and all the problems associated with writing it, go my never properly admitted thanks.

Chronology

1910   Charles Olson born 27 December in Worcester, Massachusetts.

1928   Wins third prize, a 10-week trip to Europe, in the National Oratorical Contest.

1928–1933   Attends Wesleyan University: B.A. 1932

1929   In summer attends the Gloucester School of the Little Theater; takes dance lessons with Constance Taylor.

1933   Takes graduate courses at Yale (Olin Fellowship); receives M.A. from Wesleyan University—thesis: "The Growth of Herman Melville, Prose Writer and Poetic Thinker."

1934   Father's death.

1934–1936   Instructor at Clark University, Worcester.

1936–1939   Attends Harvard as doctoral candidate first in English and American Literature, then in new American Civilization program.

1936   Friendship with Edward Dahlberg begins.

1938   "Lear and Moby Dick" (essay) published in *Twice-a-Year.*

1939   Leaves Harvard without submitting a dissertation; receives Guggenheim Fellowship for Melville studies.

1941   Publicity director for the American Civil Liberties Union, chief of the Foreign Language Information Service, Common Council for American Unity.

1942   Marries Constance Mathilde Wilcock; in September becomes associate chief of the Foreign Language Division in the Office of War Information.

1944   Director of Foreign Nationalities Division of the Democratic National Committee.

1946   In January begins visiting Ezra Pound at St. Elizabeths Hospital; sees him regularly until 1948; essay in defense of Ezra Pound. "This Is Yeats Speaking," in *Partisan Review.*

1947 *Call Me Ishmael* published.

1948 Guggenheim Fellowship for a study of the interaction of racial groups results in "Red, White & Black"; *Y & X* published by Black Sun Press; invited to Black Mountain College by Rector Josef Albers.

1949 Directs a theater program at Black Mountain.

1950 "Projective Verse" (essay) appears in *Poetry New York;* mother dies on Christmas day; goes to Mexico to study Mayan culture.

1951 Remains in Mexico until July; returns to United States to become rector of Black Mountain College.

1953 *In Cold Hell, in Thicket.*

1956 Black Mountain College closes; Olson remains in North Carolina to sell property to a retirement community.

1957 Returns in July to Gloucester, Massachusetts, summer home of his childhood.

1960 Represented in Donald Allen's *The New American Poetry, 1945–1960;* first selection of poems, *Distances; The Maximus Poems* (1–22).

1961 Experiments with Timothy Leary taking consciousness-altering drugs; *Maximus Poems IV, V, VI* completed.

1963 Teaches American poetry and mythology at State University of New York at Buffalo.

1965 *Human Universe and Other Essays* published, edited by Donald Allen; awarded the Oscar Blumenthal-Charles Leviton Prize by *Poetry* magazine.

1966 Spends five months in England, doing research for the next *Maximus* sequence, especially on the early history of Dorchester fishermen; *Selected Writings,* edited by Robert Creeley, and *Maximus IV, V, VI* published.

1969 Teaches in English Department of the University of Connecticut.

1970 Dies in New York Hospital 10 January.

1971 *Archaeologist of Morning.*

1974 *Additional Prose.*

Chapter One

Background

A poet "is made up of three parts," Charles Olson said one Friday night in July 1965, at Berkeley's Wheeler Hall, "his life, his mouth, his poem."[1] Let us begin with the life.

Born 27 December 1910 in Worcester, Massachusetts, Charles Olson was the son of a Swedish letter carrier and a Catholic Irish-American mother. The family summered in and eventually moved to Gloucester, where Charles, too, was a substitute mailman when on vacation from school. "[A]m ex-letter-carrier, ex-fisherman, ex-character," he wrote in April 1950, in his first letter to Robert Creeley.[2] He was "uneducated" at various universities: Wesleyan, Yale, and Harvard. Receiving his bachelor's and master's degrees from Wesleyan, he began teaching at Clark University as an instructor. In the summer of 1936 he went on a swordfishing cruise on the *Doris M. Hawes* into the North Atlantic to get acquainted with the fisherman's world of the sea. He was "Finding out for himself," he would later insist. The sea, although not his "trade," remained a constant obsession, drawing him to Melville and finally to the old fishing town of Gloucester.

One who paradoxically "hath not th'advantage," he finished his "uneducation" at Harvard first as a graduate student in English and American literature, and then as one of the first students enrolled in the new American Civilization program. He studied with Frederick Merk and F. O. Matthiessen. As a member of the Harvard Film Society, he supplied the commentaries on film nights while his fellow student Leonard Bernstein played the piano. Having completed the course work for his Ph.D. in American Civilization, he broke down over the endless revisions of his manuscript "Lear and Moby Dick." He received a Guggenheim Fellowship to study Melville in 1939. After finally completing his 400-page Melville study, his friend and mentor Edward Dahlberg convinced him not to publish it. A few years later, however, his *Call Me Ishmael* flowered out of it.

He took a job as publicity director for the American Civil Liberties Union (ACLU) in New York in 1941. He married Constance Mathilde

Wilcock in 1942 and in September they moved to Washington, where Olson worked for the Office of War Information. He soon rose to the position of associate chief of the Foreign Language Division. In May 1944 he became the director of the Foreign Nationalities Division of the Democratic party's National Committee. His job was to protect the rights of ethnic minorities, especially foreign nationals and racial minorities. He began writing poetry early in 1945 while spending the winter in Key West, Florida, at the Democratic party's winter quarters. Upon returning to Washington on 13 April, he learned about Roosevelt's death, which for Olson meant the death of the grand old tradition of Jeffersonianism. For a while he played with the idea of accepting posts such as assistant secretary of the Teasury or postmaster general, but then he decided to resign. After five years in politics, he gave up his public career. He started *Call Me Ishmael* the afternoon of Roosevelt's death: "that afternoon I kissed off my political future," he wrote.[3]

In 1946 he defended Ezra Pound against charges of treason ("This Is Yeats Speaking") and was commissioned by Dorothy Norman to cover Pound's trial for *Twice-a-Year*. Until 1948 he paid regular visits to Pound at St. Elizabeth's Hospital in Washington and brought comfort and sympathy to the old poet.

Between 1947 and 1951 he lectured at the University of Washington in Seattle, American University in Washington, D.C., and at Black Mountain College, in western North Carolina. During these years he established his intellectual ties: with the writer Edward Dahlberg, the anthropologist Carl Sauer, the poets Robert Duncan and Robert Creeley, and the artist Corrado Cagli. Olson spent a brief period at Black Mountain in the fall of 1948, at the invitation of Josef Albers, the rector of the college, to replace Edward Dahlberg. During the following years he returned irregularly, doing some teaching in the summer and fall of 1949, giving occasional lectures in 1950. This was a period of intensive intellectual activity, culminating in his essay "Projective Verse."

Olson was thirsty for events to happen directly to him. In December 1950 he traveled to Mexico to study Mayan civilization. Much like Melville in Polynesia, he daily observed the alien culture of a non-European civilization, devoting particular attention to experiences different from those typical of European-American culture. He stayed in Mexico until July 1951, then returned straight to Black Mountain, where he served as rector of the college from 1951 until its closing in 1956.

After the closing of the college he settled down in Gloucester and lived in poverty with his second wife, the once-brilliant actress and pianist Betty Kaiser, and their son, Charles Peter. He spent two years teaching at SUNY Buffalo, but suddenly resigned after the death of Betty in a car accident during the winter of 1964. From then until the end of his life he resided in Gloucester (except for a few months teaching at Storrs, Connecticut, in the fall of 1969). Having lost half of his weight, he died of liver cancer in 1970, at 59, hardly refuting the "fatal male small span" of the family. His last word was "wonderful."

Today, he would be happy to know his house at Fort Point is a landmark of the town, proudly listed in the *Gloucester Guide*.

Charles Olson was a mountain of a man who stood almost 6'9" tall. To some he "*was* the biggest man in the world, . . . a vast energetic spectacle."[4] Edward Dahlberg saluted his physical dimensions: "I regard your large, Jovean, laughing face with the greatest esteem and affection, and believe in your Behemoth dimensions. You are an extraordinary, gluttonous human animal."[5] "Gluttonous" in more than one respect, for Olson was an obsessive consumer of food and thought. "[Y]ou took large amounts of the refrigerator's contents to bed with you," Charles Boer recalled in his memoir of Olson (written in the moving vocative form), "everything from a jug of orange juice, a quart of ginger ale, candy, a head of lettuce to a box of crackers, cheese and hard-boiled eggs. . . . I remember well that first night, after you had finally gone to bed (the whole ritual could take hours) hearing you in the next room furiously turning the pages of the books, munching vigorously on the lettuce and other food. Every few hours that night I was suddenly awakened by a new burst of frantic munching and page-turning. It went on all night" (Boer, 24–25).

Olson was famous for being a big talker. He was totally in agreement with another famous poet, Ezra Pound, who confessed: "All my life I thought I had something to say." Socrates and Christ too "talked like mad," living "a life of talk" (*Muthologos,* 1:12). In Olson's case it was talking and reading; friends and books filled his days. "There was no sane man who could match Olson as a talker," Charles Boer remembered. "And how you talked! You knew the words that everyone wanted to hear. Who can say what you really were: a father in heaven? an honest-to-god prehistoric poet in the flesh in plastic fantastic America? a man who had all the answers?" (Boer, 33, 70). His interminable conversations were the most direct instances of his spontaneous creativity. He needed to talk in order to write; orality was, for Olson, a foundation essential to writing.

With the memory of a computer, he recalled all information he had acquired. His speech was dictated by the rapid associations that characterize his poetry. He was "a central clearing house for poetic information," as Joel Oppenheimer put it.[6] Unlike Dostoyevsky and Fellow Black Mountain poet Robert Duncan, who kept notebooks, Olson relied exclusively on his memory. In an interview he gave in Gloucester in 1968, he referred to the concept of *samtal,* or conversation, that he borrowed from Muslim poets, meaning the kind of improvised conversations where logic, classification, and Aristotelian taxonomy have no place. Instead, we have a seemingly unstructured conglomerate of ideas, expressing, in his words, the "connective necessity of a human being" (*Muthologos,* 2:89). Orality, speech, for Olson, was a means to internalize experience and to recover society's attention to the human being: "to purchase forever whatever occurs" (*Muthologos,* 2:93). The "saturation job," he called it, a method for fully enacting the moment. He talked and read poems out loud with intensity, "right up to filling every letter and word." He pictured his own reading as "the words felt as though they were made of each of the fullness of each of the letters" (*Muthologos,* 2:98).

Olson was also an obsessive reader, a "bookish man, with a wildly diverse taste for books," Ann Charters pointed out. For him reading and writing were parts of the same process. "Charles is just like I am," Robert Duncan recalled: "He sits around and reads all day."[7] An animal-like curiosity dictated his book consumption; for him, reading was a manifestation of attention and a compulsion to understand. Reading brought Olson an intimacy with the world, and especially a familiarity with history—not simply abstract knowledge, but a personal involvement, a contact with the local, a descent to the ground of the "American grain" of William Carlos Williams.

Olson's extraordinary body size was properly matched by the vastness of his spirit and personality. He was not only Maximus of Gloucester, but also the true authority and prophet for generations of American poets. He was a Socratic figure, an overpowering master, the heartbeat and catalyst of poetic movements, university departments, or residential communities, always in charge of the place he happened to be in.

The reminiscences of his students and friends abound in praise and enthusiastic assessments. Most inevitably "ended up loving the man" (Duberman, 371). William Moebius, Olson's student at Buffalo, de-

scribes him as an "elemental phenomenon such as men hold in rever-
ence, even without understanding its laws."[8] He was a charismatic
figure of great spiritual and intellectual force, a "Leviathan,"[9] who
exerted a transforming power on students, friends, the poetic scene,
and midcentury artistic sensibility. "He was an optimistic man," Fielding Dawson wrote, "he knew great expectations, and . . . [could] react
as he said like a girl, . . . catching himself before a blush. . . .
laughed in a rush, wide-eyed (remember Olson wide-eyed?) breathed
words as no one else— . . . Interested in men in ways no one else has
detailed, and each way gave true measure to a dream and his particular
dogma."[10] He was a true teacher, with the "ability to draw out of you
the very best that's in you," Michael Rumaker, the poet-student at
Black Mountain wrote; "a magician . . . Charles had a way of getting
into your unconscious . . . things that he would say would stay with
me for months and months and years and years. . . . Almost, I would
say, a compleat man . . . we were so much under the marvelous spell of
this man who was so, to us, full of life . . . a very rich kind of father
image. I was in awe of him" (Duberman, 379, 381). Olson "taught
you," in Ed Dorn's words, "to live your life with some assurance that
you are alive, forever."[11]

Apprenticeship: Fathers and Masters

What you are is what you took from others. As new tree reaches out of
compost.[12]

Olson began to write relatively late, after he had reached his intellectual maturity. By this time he had enjoyed the enriching parentage of
several mentors and spiritual forefathers. He himself talked about five
fathers: John Finch, his roommate at Wesleyan; Melville, his first literary passion; Edward Dahlberg, his closest friend during his late twenties
and early thirties; Corrado Cagli, an Italian painter who lived in America
from 1938 to 1948, whose paintings hung in Olson's house (Seelye,
xxiii). To Tom Meddick, his neighbor in Gloucester, he gave another list
of five fathers later, in 1969: Carl Olson, his real father; Wilbert Snow,
his friend and professor of English at Wesleyan; Lou Douglas, a fisherman in Gloucester; Carl Sauer, professor of geography at the University
of California, whom he met during his trip to the West Coast in 1947;
and Ezra Pound, the maestro (Boer, 87). Also, there were the fathers who
taught him at Harvard, together with Franklin Roosevelt, D. H. Law-

rence, and William Carlos Williams—all of them were his seniors and spiritual father figures. Eventually, he was to outgrow these fathers *as* fathers, and set his relationships with them on equal terms; he expected them to accept him as an intellectual partner. He confesses his torments while trying to grow out from under the shadows of his many fathers and his unwillingness to remain a son forever in a journal entry of 1948: "it is mere son I have been till now. (the way I have leaned on each of men mentioned for direction of work, decisions, gone to them to prime the pump. . . . The price I have paid is the *resistance* to them, which has racked me—the pathetic struggle to keep my own ego above their water. . . . the character of this resistance is this: I would rather be less than I dream myself to be & to be myself than any longer strive to be something each of these men could admire" (Seelye, xxiii–xxiv). He realized the harm of maintaining pupil/master relationships at the time when he was already in possession of the spiritual and imaginative legacy the fathers had to give/pass on.

Let us examine the most determining influences.

Carl Olson   Born in Sweden in 1882, he came to America when only a few months old. Most of his life he was a letter carrier in Worcester, where he knew everyone. He was "the postman," "more intimate to the community, and the lives of all the people, than anyone else could be."[13]

Olson wrote three stories about his father, "The Stocking Cap," "Mr. Meyer," and "The Post Office," describing him with love and under-standing as a man who had shy and modest friends, who liked "going free, getting out to the sensations of life" (*Post Office*, 43). Carl Olson had an immigrant's love for America and took his son to Plymouth to see the 300th anniversary celebration of the Pilgrim landing. He influ-enced his son's sense of the past by giving him Matthew Brady's *Photographic History*, thereby curing him early of romanticizing history. The father had a sense of workingmen's rights, and tried to unionize the postal workers in Worcester. When his bosses punished him, he fought back with dignity and stubbornness. "From then on," Olson tells us, "he localized his interest to the past of Gloucester and the fishing industry. . . . That was a more useable, economic America than the society of the rights of man which failed him" (*Post Office*, 28). The last story closes with the self-tormenting description of the final encounter between father and son, as the son refuses to lend him his suitcase when the father is leaving for the National Convention of Letter Carriers in

Cleveland. A few days later the father has a stroke, and dies without talking to his son again. The silence and guilt stays with him through his life. The story had to be written.

Edward Dahlberg

. . . to whom I owe all that I am in arts, all that I know.[14]

Olson met Edward Dahlberg in the summer of 1936 by looking him up at his boardinghouse in Rockport. Ten years older than Olson, Dahlberg was at the time a writer of some fame in the literary Left of New York, having published four novels, among them one, *Bottom Dogs,* with a preface by D. H. Lawrence, and another, *Those Who Perish,* the first anti-Nazi novel written in America. Olson and Dahlberg instantly developed a charged intimacy, a deep friendship built on very similar convictions about the essence of the American spirit. Equally demonic and cerebral, they seemed to have had, as Paul Christensen wrote, "one mind between them in their outlook on the past and future, with the precious difference of Dahlberg's age and literary seniority over his wonderful protégé, Charles." Dahlberg taught Olson to go slowly, to take the time for reading and learning. This was his teaching: "to write one held the book of the ancient world in your left hand and in your right you proceeded to say things that would last longer, if you only could."[15]

Dahlberg was a strict mentor, not allowing his pupil any room for deviation: he expected blind obedience. Olson felt increasingly restrained under the patriarchal authority of Dahlberg, and in his first version of the Melville book he was incapable of liberating himself from his mentor's style. Frustrated, he decided to quit writing and go into politics; so he left New York for Washington in 1941. Later, after his years in politics, when he turned to writing again, this time as a poetic apprentice to Exra Pound, Dahlberg was deeply hurt. But when Olson finished *Ishmael,* Dahlberg felt victorious: he believed it was a book that he himself had "fathered," that had been written under the domination of his identity. However, reading Olson's dedication to his real father, he felt cheated again: "I took you into my identity, gave you my table, and whatever knowledge had come to me from hunger and all the mortal and perfidious aches, you have bequeathed the volume to your poor, dead Father. . . . You have not been a Judas to me; that is a warm-livered error; your sin toward your nature and me is of a cold, stygian decoction" (17 April 1947). Bitter and wanting to cause pain, he knew no limit in his accusations, not restraining himself from pathetic curses and cruel damnations: "May God make Charles Olson a failure, may his *Call Me Ishmael* go as unsold and as unread as Thoreau and Herman Melville" (25 April 1947).

What broke their friendship was Olson's poetic development. Dahlberg could not praise his poems seeing, as he did, the influence of the new father on them, the one who had succeeded Dahlberg in feeding Olson's spirit: Ezra Pound. "[T]he difference between *CALL ME ISHMAEL* and *Y & X* is the ultimate distinction between Edward Dahlberg and Ezra Pound," Dahlberg pointed out in bitter disappointment (18 January 1949). Disagreements became more common, leaving less and less ground for understanding and shared beliefs. By 1950 Olson had reached his full artistic maturity, where Dahlberg could not follow him, although Olson gave him credit in several places, most notably in "Projective Verse." At this time Olson, going his own way, developed with Robert Creeley and Cid Corman two alliances that would shape and determine his career. After Olson established himself firmly at Black Mountain the estrangement between him and Dahlberg widened. Olson's refusal to write a critique of Dahlberg's *The Flea of Sodom,* a refusal based on his inability to give it a positive assessment, caused emotional pain to both parties and finally ended their friendship. In his last letter to Dahlberg Olson asked him to "go aside, go aside" (18 November 1955). After 1955 they never communicated again; they parted in "a rebuke, in love, in sorrow" (Dahlberg's final letter, 24 November 1955).

Ezra Pound   For a writer serving his apprentice years as self-consciously as Olson was in the 1940s, Pound was an obvious choice as mentor. Olson wrote two poems on Pound, and defended him before the trial in November 1945. Employing the voice of William Butler Yeats, who had died in 1939, Olson set forth an argument in which he avoided politics (he himself was appalled by the older poet's views on fascism), but inspected Pound's situation from the point of view of artistic merit and posterity. Poets, he stated as the first rule, should stay out of politics. Although he was outraged by Pound's views on class and race superiority, he felt he knew exactly what Pound's poetic worth was to America. And that worth could be measured by no court; only history could judge: "There is a court you leave silent—history present, the issue the larger concerns of authority than state, . . . , perhaps some consideration of descents and metamorphoses, form and the elimination of intellect. . . . Are you a court to accept and/or reject JEFFERSON AND/OR MUSSOLINI, indict GUIDE TO CULTURE and write a better, brief me contrary ABCs, charge why 100 CANTOS betrays your country, that poem which concerns itself so much with the men who made your Revolution for you? . . . What do you find, a traitor?" (Seelye, 30–31). He also raised a warning against the moral dangers of organized hypocrisy: "The soul is stunned in me, o writers, readers, fighters, fearers, . . . that you have allowed this to happen without a trial of your own. . . . What have you to hold in a single thought reality and justice?" (Seelye, 30–31).

Olson was commissioned to cover the Pound trial for *Twice-a-Year.* In his reports he gave a picture of the personal drama of the man cornered in a court. He admired Pound's strength of curiosity even while imprisoned in the "Gorilla Cage" at Pisa. Olson's relation to Pound was complex: he both hated him for being an anti-Semite and a traitor and yet tried to understand his idiosyncratic interpretation of his civil responsibility and his ill-fated attempt to save the American constitution: "Poor, poor Pound, the great gift, the true intellectual, rotting away, being confined and maltreated by the Administration. SHIT" (Seelye, 48–49).

Olson visited Pound at St. Elizabeths Hospital for a period of two and a half years. They developed a deep, relaxed, gentle relationship. Olson was basically trying to ease Pound's days by helping him with various chores. After the trial their conversations turned more and more to writing. Pound was an animated reader of Olson's poems; giving him much encouragement through his comments. He was impressed by *Call Me Ishmael,* too, and helped Olson find a publisher for it. Olson mentioned once that he had "stolen" a poem from him. "At which," as Olson reports, "he made a gesture like a salute with the right hand, as much as to say, take it away" (Seelye, 69). The disciple grown up, the spiritual alliance was perfected.

Black Mountain College

I'm a Professor of Posture, and I'm proving it. (*Muthologos,* 1:123)

Olson liked to see himself as a "Professor of Posture," with the larger purpose of acquainting his students with all that he himself had learned. *Posture* seems to be the exact word, the common denominator of all that Olson ever taught through his poems and essays, lectures on philosophy and mathematics, archaeology and history during the five years he taught, 1951–56, at Black Mountain College.

"A pioneer adventure,"[16] Black Mountain College was an experimental educational workshop, particularly in the fields of literature and the arts. As an American Bauhaus, it was, as Chad Walsh suggested in 1968, "probably the most influential college that has collapsed in America during the past thirty years" (*Muthologos,* 2:55). It was in existence for 23 years, 1933–56, during which time it was the home, inspiration, and refuge of some of the most extraordinary innovative talents of our time: the founder philosopher John Rice; the German constructivist artist and art historian Josef Albers, and his wife, the artist and weaver Anni Albers; the poet Charles Olson; the composer and mixed media performer John Cage, together with his close associate, the pianist and composer David Tudor; the modern dancer and choreographer Merce Cunningham; the abstract expressionists Franz Kline, Willem de Kooning, and Arshile Gorky; the "comprehensive designer" Buckminister Fuller; the collage artist Robert Rauschenberg; the beloved conductor and musicologist Heinrich Jalowetz from Vienna. The poets associated with Black Mountain College included Robert Duncan, Robert Creeley, Paul Goodman, Cid Corman, Ed Dorn, Michael Rumaker, Leroi Jones (lmamu Amiri Baraka), Joel Oppenheimer, John Wieners, Jonathan Williams, and Fielding Dawson. Prominent visitors included philosopher and education reformer John Dewey, authors Thornton Wilder and Henry Miller, writer and philosopher Aldous Huxley, architect, designer, and founder of the Bauhaus Walter Gropius, action painters Robert Motherwell and Jackson Pollock, Alan Kaprow, the creator of the happening, and counterculture ideologist Lewis Mumford.

The college began with the dismissal of eight faculty members from Rollins College in Winter Park, Florida, including John Andrew Rice, who were accused of " 'irrelevant discussions' on sex, religion and 'unconventional living' " (Duberman, 22). Four of the faculty members, concerned about their students, decided to start a new college, and found an ideal site for it on the low hills of Black Mountain, North Carolina. It was a place pregnant with the myth of the "wilderness," offering a possibility for the realization of the utopian dream of an intellectual and spiritual commune.

The college was based on some basic principles: openness, personal freedom, experimental and workshop spirit, self-sufficiency, equality, common responsibility. As a democratic place, it respected only a "hierarchy based on talent, toughness, intelligence and honesty" (Duberman, 407). The community allowed each individual a measure of privacy, but faculty and students lived communally, worked the land or fought forest fires, ate their meals and performed together. All operations were conducted in one building, the Robert E. Hall. Teaching was not restricted to the classroom or to classroom hours, but went on everywhere day and night. Living and learning were not separate activities, nor was any distinction made between "curricular" and "extracurricular" activities. The students were involved in the decision making and shared the responsibility for running the college. Few rules were codified; Black Mountain had an ethos, a spirit, not a rule book. Black Mountain was pioneering in another respect too: it was then the only Southern College that admitted both whites and blacks. At the college the educational principles of John Dewey combined with the spirit of European modernism carried there by artists and scholars fleeing fascism in Europe.

The community was never larger than 150 people, faculty included. There was an insistence on self-sufficiecy ("housekeeping"): the college had its own cooperative store and print shop, together with 600 acres of farm land. Students and faculty worked together to run the farm, growing crops, raising cattle, chickens, and pigs. In consequence of the "work program" of the school, this farm produced 60 percent of the community's food. Instead of being employed by the college, the teachers "shared" it. Basically they were given food and shelter; after the college was sold, they were paid a percentage of the proceeds based on the amount of time they had taught there. Olson recalled that "the founding of Black Mountain was based upon these principles: no accreditation, no board of trustees, no endowment, no ranks—all people payed the same and one payment for everybody" (*Muthologos,* 2:62–63). As Olson explained: "A diverse group of people taught and studied here, sharing only intellectualism and radicalism and the commitment to something different. An air of mystery surrounds the college today, but that mystery seems to have been there from the start: 'the gracefulness, the enormous gracefulness, and the complete unsafety, . . . the total insecurity, founded, built in, created in its origin, and this incredible gracefulness of human condition' " (Olson's interview, in *Muthologos,* 2:57).

As to the curriculum, there are "no fixed regulations at Black Mountain—no required courses, no systems of frequent examinations, no formal grading. For the first ten days of classes, students were encouraged to 'shop around,' to sit in on classes, sample possibilities, and then decide on a schedule. Responsibility . . . was placed on the student himself for deciding what shape his education should take" (Duberman, 49). Rarely were the individual classes conducted according to a preset program, but room was purposely left for impromptu discussions. Rice believed in a participatory atmosphere, "in letting each class session find its immediate interest . . . and pursuing that interest wherever it led and however long it took" (Duberman, 22).

Josef and Anni Albers came from the Bauhaus in Berlin and brought with them—apart from a hunger for experimentation—qualities such as discipline, diligence, and precision. They believed in training the consciousness in art as the chief vehicle for individual growth, and in teaching the creative process by encouraging sight and articulation even in those who did not consider themselves particularly gifted. "I want to open eyes" was one of Josef Albers's first sentences in English, and the "heart of his message" (Duberman, 59).

Olson first arrived as a surrogate for Edward Dahlberg, who had found the natural setting "murderous" and was incapable of getting along with the students. Olson, "the tallest and most powerful vocal antenna on campus,"[17] immediately became a "cult figure," who "came on—at Black Mountain as everywhere—like a force of nature. His enormous size, energy and verbal pyrotechnics made him instantly impressive. . . . as a replacement and transient, Olson entered a community that he was soon to dominate—and continue to dominate— until it closed its doors in 1956" (Duberman, 308). Olson continued directing the college in the spirit of education inherited from the founders. "I came with no ideas; Black Mountain did it all," he said to emphasize the existing spirit of the place. In the 1952 spring semester catalog he insisted on teaching as a free exchange of ideas, following John Rice's educational principles:

Our central and consistent effort is to teach method, not content; to emphasize process. . . . The law of the teacher at Black Mountain is to function as a working "artist" . . . to be no passive recipient or hander-out of mere information. . . . There are subtle means of communication that have been lost by mankind as our nerve ends have been cauterized by schooling. To learn to move, at least without fear, to fear, see, touch, also without fear . . . to be aware of everything around us . . . this is to start to penetrate the past and to *feel* as well as mentally see our way into the future.[18]

Olson, a most persuasive teacher, wanted to change the visions of his students. Duncan tells us that for Olson education was a "kind of spiritual attack. . . . He wanted things to happen in them spiritually."[19] John Cech supports this view of Olson's endeavor: "He had one object: he was out to convert your soul, at least to compel the awareness that you had one and that it sang and cried."[20] During Olson's years of administration, classes were held according to the inner rhythm of the teachers. Duncan's rhythm was morning; whereas Olson's was evening and night. Often Olsen lead marathon classes running as long as 24 hours. The spirit was free, or organic rather, following an inner rhythm, *in order to* create an ideal working situation for students and teachers. Robert Creeley recalls having to give his first class immediately after arriving at Black Mountain after several days' traveling; he also tells us how students insistent on learning would physically take him to class, saying "We're here to be taught."[21]

With Olson as rector, the college turned into the "arts center" Albers had insisted on, although the emphasis shifted from the visual to the verbal arts. It was now a distinctive place attracting people who had formulated their visions and philosophy of action around ideas of process and energy, field, personal voice, randomness, spontaneity, playfulness, primitive or preliterate traditions. For them it was an ideal place for poets, a "camp" of "alive people," as Ed Dorn put it (*Muthologos*, 1:174–75), of artists living in fellowship and community. Through the workshop atmosphere, Black Mountain provided a creative context for teacher and poet alike, a learning environment where one could belong. Gerard van der Wiele's sentiments were not uncommon: "I don't believe I ever in my life felt that I belonged any place as much as I felt I belonged at that school" (Duberman, 407). A "beloved community," Black Mountain prefigured the sixties counterculture in many respects. Above all, it was a "live" community: it gave, in Olson's words, "that condition of liveliness," when "you feel you're not asleep" (*Muthologos*, 2:77). Olson always insisted that it was a "polis," a true communal city. "A city is a wonderful thing," he recalled, "because you can walk in and out of it, yes? At the same time, it is a unit" (*Muthologos*, 2:69). Indeed, at its height, Black Mountain was a spiritual unit that allowed one the freedom of walking in or out, yet at the same time magnetized all its members into coherence, giving them a sense of belonging there together. When the college was finally closed down, this great ark of fellowship was broken and the disciples scattered all over the world.

But forever "the seeds live inside you," Eliot Weinberger confessed (Duberman, 412).

Although Olson himself did not like the label "Black Mountain poets," he recognized that the binding force of the Black Mountain spirit was strong enough to keep a "bunch of pre-metaphysical conceitists" (*Muthologos,* 2:82) like himself, Duncan, Creeley, and Dorn together. It is to these poets that Olson was referring when he said: "I got about five people who have given me any evidence that they know what the fuck I said" (*Muthologos,* 2:130). Their bond was the common aesthetics and common training they gave and received at Black Mountain. Many of the ideas shared by the group—Olson, Creeley, Duncan, Levertov, and Dorn, as well as Cid Corman, Michael Rumaker, Joel Oppenheimer, Jonathan Williams, Leroi Jones, Fielding Dawson, and others—had been formulated by Olson. William Aiken goes as far as suggesting that Black Mountain might be "regarded as a kind of Corinth for the early Olson community. . . . after a certain time, Olson in the figure of Maximus, like Paul of Tarsus, begins to communicate in letters, sent out to growing projective communities."[22] In his perennial concern for the artistic salvation of others, Olson had the spiritual capacity, the inner radiance that granted him such a prophetic role.

Chapter Two

"Projective Verse" and "Human Universe"

"Projective Verse"

> i wish very much, Creeley, I had now to send you what PNY
> [*Poetry New York*] publishes summer issue, *PROjective Verse vs. the
> NON-projective:* the argument pitches here
>   (I've dubbed the alternative to composing by inherited forms
> "composition by field"—it needs more examination than I give
> it, in that kick-off piece.
>
> *(Olson-Creeley Correspondence,* 1:19)

The year is 1950, and Olson is announcing to Creeley the forthcoming publication, in *Poetry New York,* of his essay "Projective Verse," a "kick-off piece." Indeed, this "kick-off piece" has become one of the most studied and debated poetic manifestos of the century.

"Projective Verse" was Olson's first and major *ars poetica,* his credo of poetic technique and philosophy that influenced a whole generation of poets. It became his most anthologized piece; more than any of his writings, poetry or prose, this essay has won academic attention, entered the pantheon: it has become an integral part of twentieth-century American literature syllabi. It has, in the four decades of its lifetime, been applauded, canonized, glorified, paraphrased, popularized, plagiarized debased, parodied, made fun of—everything but ignored or forgotten.

The essay falls into two distinct parts, as Olson himself explains, doing two things: talking about *technical* and *philosophical* questions. The technical issues involve various dogmas relating to *projective or open verse* and *composition by field.* The dogmas refer to the *kinetics* of writing (poem as energy), *form as an extension of content,* the *process* of composition, and the *material/linguistic elements* of the open poem dependent on and expressive of breath and speech. The philosophical issues relate to the "stance towards reality" that projective writing involves. Concepts such as objectism, obeyance, attention, humilitas, and participation contribute to the definition of this Olsonian "posture."

Part 1

Dogma #1

In Dogma #1 ("the *kinetics* of the thing"—in "composition by field") Olson insists that some "simplicities" are to be learned. The first among them is the manifestation of the kinetics of composition, the concept of the poem as energy-construct: "a poem is energy transferred from where the poet got it (he will have some several causations), by way of them poem itself to, all the way over to, the reader. . . . Then the poem itself must, at all points, be a high energy-construct and, at all points, an energy discharge."[1]

The writing situation is predominantly defined by openness: the poet must make a conscious effort to remain as open as possible to the energy forces around himself; he gathers and transmits these spiritual and material energies as he writes the poem. The poem is thus a transfer of energy, and as such has a kinetic nature. "This means very literally," Creeley explains, "that a poem is some *thing,* a structure possessed of its own organization in turn derived from the circumstances of its making."[2] Put boldly, the "going out" (writing) is the direct continuation or extension of the "coming in" (perception).

Olson's stress on the kinetic properties of the poem, as well as his idea of composition by field, has a family resemblance to some ideas of William Carlos Williams, such as his reliance on physical influences at work during composition, even such influences as the pace of walking, that seemed to have little to do with poetry writing. In his 1948 essay "The Poem as a Field of Action," Williams insisted on a new measure for the poem commensurate with the world as redefined by Einstein's theory of relativity; he speaks of the poem as a "category of activity" and as a possibility for discoveries made by listening to the language.[3] The founding of a poetics on a theory of perception supported by modern scientific thought (Einstein and Whitehead) seems also to have come to Olson via Williams.

But Williams was not his only source of inspiration. Thomas F. Merrill points to the kinship between Olson's Dogma #1 and "Fenollosa's concept of the sentence as a 'transference of power' applied to verse," as well as to the fact that Williams *and* Pound had developed the concept of the poem as "energy-construct" years before Olson, though with less emphasis. The epistemological position implied by this dogma reveals, Merrill goes on, "hints of influence of Whitehead, Jung, and even Merleau-Ponty to come."[4] While Olson was specifying the "technical" details of his poetics, he was, it seems, also engaged in the articulation of a grander philosophy. "Olson's comprehensive stance," Merrill claims, "involves the status of man (be he poet or not) in relation to his environment" (49).

Dogma #2

Dogma #2 ("form is never more than an extension of content") is the "principle" that is the rephrasing of organic form, Coleridge's "Form as Proceeding," as opposed to a priori form, or "Shape Superinduced." Form that is an *extension* of content claims simultaneity of content and form, as well as of self and world in its refusal to use a preexisting form, or a form that precedes (and by doing so kills) experience and idea. Olson gives credit to Creeley for the phrasing, and indeed we do find the idea in Creeley's letters right before the publication of "Projective Verse." Here is one passage, for example, that abounds in usable references: "The 'formal' has killed what the head: might get into: in that it has put into menial/ enclosed/ work: what it sd have been determining, ONLY as an extension of its center: in any given work. Which is to say: as now, in many, the insistence on an attention (FIRST) to possible castings for a content" (*Olson-Creeley Correspondence*, 1:63). Here Creeley is insisting on the value of attention and a free flow of feeling, as opposed to formal control, which generates an enclosed work. The poem this law produces shall differ in a very fundamental way from the closed, self-sufficient, unified poem exalted by New Critical canon-makers of the time.

Explicating Olson's second dogma, Thomas F. Merrill says that "Man should resist imposing his forms egotistically upon Nature as a matter of perceptual propriety" (49). Indeed, Olson is attacking the assumptions that form is a preexisting given or even something that the poet consciously makes, assumptions founded on the philosophical principle that self is divided from world. Paul Christensen explains that "Olson refers to this principle in the essay only to suggest that traditional forms are imposed by conventions which preserve the separations of self and world: the poet is asked to change the shape of his feelings to conform to certain uniform expectations of poetic response."[5] Once again Olson is taking up arms against the old controlling humanism. For the old techniques of employing traditional forms or consciously setting out to create new forms, Olson substitutes *projectivism:* "You enter the subject matter, and *that* projection is where you permit your feeling to flow and go out through the subject matter" (*Muthologos,* 1:184).

Charles Altieri emphasizes that unlike those (especially those trained in New Criticism,) for whom the famous formula on form as an extension of content is self-evident and even commonplace, Olson took the formula in a literal way: for him, form is a *dynamic union of world and acting agent* realized in attention and humility, not by means of *creative imposition.* "Form is literally within the event as dynamic union of world and acting agent; in no way is it the structuring of an event by a responding, interpreting mind. The development of western poetics illustrates for Olson the gradual realization that form is completely secular . . .—to be realized in attention and humility and not imposed by the creative mind."[6] The key terms here are "event" and "gradual realization," "union of self and world," "attention" and "humility."

The task of the poet is not to impose, but to *extend,* to *realize* content into form by acting as little as the controlling agency as possible. Attention and humility guarantee this holding back of the ego, and help form obey its inner laws. Denise Levertov's variant on the famous Olson-Creeley dogma ties in at this point: "Form is never more than a *revelation* of content."[7]

Dogma #3

"I think it can be boiled down to one statement (first pounded into my head by Edward Dahlberg): ONE PERCEPTION MUST IMMEDIATELY AND DIRECTLY LEAD TO A FURTHER PERCEPTION. . . . Get on with it, keep moving, keep in, speed . . . keep it moving as fast as you can, citizen. . . . Always one perception must must must MOVE, INSTANTER, ON ANOTHER!" (PV, 16–17). Dogma #3 ("the *process* of the thing") is Olson's version of the postmodern concept of poetic process consonant with the mechanisms of perception. Olson believed that the direct and immediate projection of sense perceptions would guarantee the kind of dynamic and open, or "willess," poetry in which kinetic energies abound. Clearly, as Olson himself acknowledged, Edward Dahlberg was responsible for this belief: the intellectual patent is his. For critics, however, the debt seems even greater than Olson allows us to believe; John Cech points out that Dahlberg is responsible not only for the phrasing of the third dogma, but also for the poetic practice Olson perfected: "Dahlberg had been instrumental in helping Olson to define the process by which the projective poet should work; and Olson took Dahlberg's advice and constant proddings about the need to avoid delay and propel himself quickly, deeply, and personally into the work at hand—transforming these personal experiences into one of the general rules of Projective Verse composition" (Cech, 111).

Among the many things that Olson inherited from Dahlberg (such as his communitarian ideals that Olson refashioned into his concept of the *polis,* as well as his eccentric methods of abbreviation and short-hand), this *principle of poetic process* seems to be the most important. This severe "discipline of progression," as Paul Christensen calls it, is the single most determining influence on his poetry: the progression "from one clarifying assertion to the next" gives his poems a certain "dizzying quality, as they race ahead of the reader's speed of comprehension, widening, molding, extending the attention by quick jerky steps in perception" (Christensen, 71–72).

Dogma #3 is not a plain rephrasing of the processural conception of creativity of postmodern poetics. It is much more than that: it is the concept that—like a key—turns on and generates the most conspicu-ous qualities of Olson's verse: its speed, its racing thoughts, its momen-tum, its unlimited intellectual courage. In an unpublished manuscript probably dating from the winter of 1945, Olson demands exactly this racing, propelling modality of his own poetry: "Leap ahead and try the ambitions. Go to the extreme of your imagination and go on from there: fail large, never succeed small. Again ED [Dalhberg] makes sense: one intuition must only lead to another farther place" (quoted in Cech, 88–89). John Cech properly terms this doctrine of Dahlberg's as one relating to "imaginative risk-taking" that Olson transformed "into a formula for accelerating composition and thus outdistancing 'ennui' " (Cech, 89).

Again, Olson transgresses the accepted domain of poetic technique in stating his dogma. As Thomas F. Merrill points out, this dictum on process is the poetical application of the ontological truth Olson learned from Riemann and Whitehead, namely, that reality is continuous rather than a discrete manifold. "[T]he expression of that reality accord-ingly should be continuous and not discrete. Thus the dogma proposes a poetic process consonant with the natural process of the universe" (Merrill, 49).

Dogma #4

With Dogma #4 ("breath allows *all* the speech force of language back in") we are "inside the machinery" (PV, 17): breath as speech force is becoming the ultimate measure of projective writing, determining its qualities in a far-reaching way. Poetry in Olson's conception, is not only a verbal but also a *physiological act,* that fuses mental and natural, biological and physical values.

Olson emphasizes the physicality of writing by locating the syllable and the line in the world of ear and mind, breath and body.

From the union of the mind and the ear the syllable is born. . . . the other child is the LINE. And together, these two, the syllable *and* the line, they make a poem. . . . And the line comes (I swear it) from the breath, from the breathing of the man who writes, at the moment that he writes . . . Let me put it boldly. The two halves are:
                  the HEAD, by way of the EAR, to the SYLLABLE
                  the HEART, by way of the BREATH, to the LINE.
                                                              (PV, 18–19)

Breath is the physical vehicle of projectivism, directly transporting what the poet perceives during the act of composition: "It is the advantage of the typewriter that, due to its rigidity and space precisions, it can, for a poet, indicate exactly the breath, the pauses, the phrases, the suspensions even of syllables, the juxtapositions even of parts of phrases, which he intends. For the first time the poet has the stave and the bar a musician has had. For the first time he can, without the convention of rime and meter, record the listening he has done to his own speech" (PV, 22). This is a technical description of the mechanics (or "machinery") of projectivism. The writer projects experience cadenced/articulated/structured by breath onto the page; breath is an essential factor in creativity. A projective poem will, as Ekbert Faas rightly puts it, "mirror in print the 'presentational immediacy' which is the poem's essence. In this way the reader . . . will relive the process of creation and share the dance of cosmic forces that has found a voice in the poem's words and rhythms."[8] The projective act will provide a release for the "flow of creation" that the poet apprehends and transmits.

Olson in the essay refers to the romantic notion of "inspiration" by quoting the "Western Wynd." This archetype of creative spirit brings breath into the making of the poem. However, the romantic concept, which itself has its roots in the Bible, when, by the magic power of God, the *Pneuma,* man became a living soul, does not quite fit Olson's stance. The word *Pneuma* took the meaning of spirit only under the influence of Christianity, but the word *spirit* has preserved a double meaning in several languages. Among primitive peoples breath is believed to be both of the body and of the spirit, both physical and spiritual in essence. Breath is recognized as "soul-substance" to be inhaled by the dying father's son in order to take over the soul, but its purely bodily nature is never doubted or ignored.

Modernism taught concentration and the importance of focusing on the materials of poetry, music, and art. Here, the qualities inherent in the more or less physical nature of the material become meaningful in an autonomous way. Olson has learned from the moderns about the breath-substance of language: "the words made solely of air," he might have read in Williams, or "the winds are under my lips" in Pound's "De Aeqypto." What is more important in this respect he took over from Pound, and quoted repeatedly, the seemingly absurd dictum that "the body is inside the soul" (Boer, 125). "I think," he said in this vein, "our body is our soul. And if you don't have your body as a factor of creation, you don't have a soul" (*Muthologos,* 2:170). Because for Olson the body is part of the soul, and vice versa, the bodily and the spiritual are aspects of one and the same process. Breath no longer serves as a metaphor for the spiritual, but becomes the *extension* of the bodily into the spiritual.

It is not hard to trace the sources of inspiration behind the four dogmas of the first part of "Projective Verse": William Carlos Williams, Ezra Pound, Edward Dahlberg, and Robert Creeley are all actively present with their ideas. But for Olson the creative tradition was more important than any individual achievement; he believed that the community of poets, artists, musicians, and thinkers shared the same mind. And Olson was not alone in this preference. Williams, for example, incorporated much of the first part of "Projective Verse" in his *Autobiography* without either seeking Olson's consent or bothering about bureaucratic copyright procedures. Olson, at first taken aback by this expression of kinship, soon realized that Williams's recognition of intellectual and imaginative camaraderie was what mattered. Williams expressed the same recognition in a letter to Creeley: "I share your excitement, it is as if the whole area lifted. It's the sort of thing we are

after and must have . . . everything in it leans on action, on the verb;
one thing *leads* to another which is thereby activated."[9]

It never bothered Olson to use other poets' ideas. "Originality" was
an ideal he nearly despised. "Use, use, use," was his imperative. Without being imitative or derivative, he was a grand and courageous synthe-
sizer; his poetry and philosophy is a treasury and storehouse of usable
ideas.

Part 2   In the second part of "Projective Verse" Olson turns to
"the degree to which the projective involves a stance toward reality
outside the poem," since the projective act, "the artist's act in the larger
field of objects, leads to dimensions larger than the man" (PV, 25).

Even as he writes, Olson is trying to find the exact name for this
stance. First he brings up "objectivism," but he is not satisfied because
the term might be misunderstood as the opposite of "subjectivism." A
"more valid formulation" is, then, *"objectism"* since it stands for a "relation of man to experience":

> *Objectism* is the getting rid of the lyrical interference of the individual as ego, of
> the "subject" of his soul, that peculiar presumption by which western man has
> interposed himself between what he is as a creature of nature (with certain
> instructions to carry out) and those other creations of nature which we may,
> with no derogation, call objects. For a man is himself an object, whatever he
> may take to be his advantages, the more likely to recognize himself as such the
> greater his advantages, particularly at the moment that he achieves an
> humilitas sufficient to make him of use (PV, 24–25).

It is, the *use* of man that Olson is interested in: of man as *object* capable of
participating with *humilitas* in nature. The use of man is determined by
"how he conceives his relation to nature, that force to which he owes his
somewhat small existence. . . . if he stays inside himself, if he is contained within his natures as he is participant in the larger force, he will be
able to listen, and his hearing through himself will give him secrets
objects share" (PV, 25). Breath, "man's special qualification as animal"
will allow him to stay inside himself, contained, with humility.

Here Olson takes a direct and explicit stand against the New Critical
canon, and especially T. S. Eliot, attacking in an iconoclastic way.
Eliot, Olson concludes, is not projective, and that is the reason why he
fails as a dramatist: "his root is the mind alone" (PV, 26). Unlike Eliot,
the projective poet does not allow the "scholastic" separation of self and

world, spiritual and physical. He will go "down through the workings of his own throat to that place where breath comes from, where breath has its beginnings, where drama has to come from, where, the coincidence is, all act springs" (PV, 26).

Part 2 presents Olson's stance toward reality, and thereby complements the more technical poetics elaborated in Part I. His far-reaching radicalism is expressed in the doctrine of objectism applied to both man and poet. Poetry is here conceived as immanent part of the larger forces of life: for Olson even the most technical issues of poetry, those relating to the "machinery" of writing, are basically philosophical—ontological, epistemological, and psychological—concerns.

Olson describes an existence where the boundaries between the subjective and the objective are dissolved, where subjectivity is transcended, where the individual is object outside of the 'ego-position.' The fruit of this existence shall be a poetry of sincerity, born of an open and alert consciousness. There is a whole field of concepts in interplay here: *obedience* (defined by Charles Altieri as "a mode of relatedness between words and world"), [10] *humility* (the transcendence of subjectivity), *participation* (the dissolving of boundaries between the subjective and the objective), *objecti(vi)sm* ("a strategy for indulging in attributions to the self as object . . . [and] to suppress in the position of subject" [Altieri, 24]), *alertness* (the eyes looking out of the head), and *perception* (the ecstasy in which man participates as a whole organism).

The Projective Stance

The physical appearance of Olson's poems, with lines scattered over the surface of the pages, broken and indented, is one mark, the most obvious one, of the projectivist stance. Projections and transcripts of the workings of his mind, Olson's poems follow in an visually perceivable way the turmoil in his mind at the moment of composition.

Robert Creeley describes this faithful adherence of the projective poem to mental energies in a letter dated July 1950: "This would seem to me to be a principal advantage of Pro Verse, OPEN FIELD, that: the *objects* which occur, at the moment of recognition (you had composition—how abt that/ same damn thing), can because of, THE SPEECH, BACK IN (the energy), be treated exactly as they do occur (in their effects, that is, on us, daily, can keep their confusions" (*Olson-Creeley Correspondence*, 2:60). For Olson, the most important creative faculties are not ordering, rethinking, systematizing, classifying, and other modes of categorizing, but listening, obeying, responding, remaining in a state of intellectual

transparency in order to be able to *transcribe* (by *projecting* onto the page)
all that surfaces within the poet at the time of writing.

The flow of this surfacing is punctuated by *breath*—physiology and
mind/intellect are not separable—in such a way that the resulting form
mirrors, through typography, spacings, and other visual devices, the
emergence of mental blocks (thoughts, ideas, etc.).

Creeley also emphasizes this coincidence of the visual and mental in
projective verse and prose:

> But you realize that it's all happening visually as well as intellectually and
> mentally. Olson, in his letters . . . you begin to realize Olson's spacing, the
> ordering of where things occur in his thought. He'll begin a letter like, "dear
> so and so," and then start with the information, and before he's, say, halfway
> through the page you've got these things jumping all around . . . the move-
> ment, is moving, trying to locate, like, let's put that there . . . no don't, now
> this goes here, oh but you can forget that . . . but you can't forget this
> too . . . you can't put them like that, because it's a lie, they don't exist that
> way, you've got to. . . . He's trying in effect to give the *orders* of thought—in
> no pretentious sense—and a typewriter for him, for example, is something
> that has much defined his habits of writing, as he himself said in "Projective
> Verse."[11]

Indeed, as Paul Christensen puts it, "the shapes and clusters are the
scoring of the poet's thought. . . . The projective poem has visual
impact on the reader: one can glance at the overall shape of the poem to
be read and know with some accuracy whether the thinking is turbu-
lent and difficult or meditative and evenly paced" (84).

For Christensen, though, projectivism means primarily *spatial prosody*. In his seminal book on Olson, he engages in a topographic study of
projective poetry around the two axes of thought and event, translating
thought and event into horizontal and vertical progression, respectively. I think this interpretation is inadequate, since projectivism
involves more than the spatial scoring of the thinking process.

The *essence* of the projective act seems to be its effort at faithfully
presenting the *process* of creation as well as its attempt, as Ekbert Faas
points out, to be "a direct release of the unceasing 'flow of creation' ":

> The poet's creativity springs from a fusion with the "flow of creation," for
> which man's original language had been the direct medium. Poetic creation
> becomes a simple release of these natural forces, in which the poet feels himself
> to be a part of the cosmos. Poetry is not made but happens, is not an abstrac-

tion that rises to transcend nature but a natural event that embodies it—what Lawrence describes as "life surging itself into utterance at its very well-head," and Olson as the poet's "projective act." (Faas, 46).

Faas points out some fundamental resemblances of this projective act to gestural or action painting, Stockhausen's meditative sound release compositions, Sino-Japanese calligraphy and *Sumi-e* painting, and Zen Buddhist flute music, all of which flow "from the autonomous spontaneity of the artist's bodily movements" or breath rhythm, "expressing man's vital harmony with the universe" (Faas, 46–47). Of course, Black Mountain College was *the* place for such experiments, with performances by John Cage, Franz Kline, Buckminster Fuller, or Charles Olson in nearly all these media. The common impulse behind the diversity represented by action painting, calligraphy, Zen Buddhist flute music, and Cage's chance operations is what Olson described as Projective Geometry: "that movement of force as wave and particle and particles dissolving into vibration" (*Muthologos,* 2:73). In other words, all these forms of creativity insist on the immediate transference of energy, on the unity of the creating and projecting gestures.

The projective impulse rejects all closed systems involving exterior and a priori patterns and models. The distinction is the same as the one Charles Altieri draws between the "optative method" and "field poetics" or "poetics of conjecture":

The optative method is characterized by an author's "particularized determined choice among possibilities" when they are subjected to the external constraints of plot, themes, verse form, metaphoric pattern, and so on, which, once chosen, dictate or at least greatly limit further specific choices. . . . In field poetics, or the poetics of conjecture and extension, on the other hand, purpose is rejected in favour of simple "paying attention," on all levels, to possibilities of thinking, that emerge as the poet opens up what is folded into some initial subject or condition. The poem is less a well-made object than an opportunity, a play of energies created by what Duncan calls the passage and crossings of mind, text, and world. (Altieri 1984, 110)

Projective Prosody

"Olson's emphasis is put on prosody, not interpretation," Creeley wrote.[12] Prosody as the spatial scoring of the thinking process is indeed of utmost significance in Olson's projective poetics. Olson accepted Williams's dictum that "the poetic line has to be opened up" from

external tightness, because it has, as Creeley observes, "more to do with
the poem's pattern than with the movement of its sense."[13]

Olson's stand against this external tightness was in consonance with
his insistence on the centrality of the poetic line in projectivist poetics.
"For Olson," Creeley emphasizes, "the line becomes a way to a movement beyond the single impact of the words which go to make it up,
and brings to their logic a force of its own. Instead of the simple wagon
which carries the load, he makes it that which drives too, to the
common logic, the sense of the poem" (Charles Olson: *Y & X*, 151–
52). It is very important that Olson's line has a "force of its own," for it
is not only the "wagon carrying the load," but the agent that "drives"
it, too. I think Creeley's description is the most exact and convincing
use of imagery to elucidate/exemplify the peculiarity of Olson's line.
Olson's line is, simultaneously, a high energy construct and an energy
discharge.

Alan Golding, in his essay on Olson's theory of free verse, gives an
illuminating and convincing overview of projective prosody. Stressing
the centrality of the line, Golding states that Olson's prosody is primarily visual: "typography becomes a major clue to rhythmic structure."[14]
Golding's close analysis of the prosodic "manner" of the poem "in Cold
Hell, in Thicket" reveals that "the argument of the prosody extends to
follow the argument of the poem, the rhythmical collage matching
Olson's thought in its complex windings until finally both prosody and
thought achieve clarity and resolution." He finds syntax of accumulation and apposition rather than conneciton in the poem, as well as other
prosodic devices like the predominance of monosyllables and a high
incidence of the use of caesura—all adding up to an "energetic forward
moving rhythm" (68) and "an intensification of attention" (69). Speed
and action are brought about by prosodic means. Going "by ear" only,
Olson realized prosody in the sense in which Pound understood the
terms ("the articulation of the total sound of the poem") and as the
ultimate possibility for *measure:*

>   I measure my song
>   measure the sources of my song,
>   measure me, measure
>   my forces

Creeley quotes Olson as he defines projective prosody in terms of *mapping* and *congruence:* "metric then is mapping, . . . congruent means of
making a statement."

"Human Universe"

Part 1   Olson wrote his second major speculative essay, "Human Universe," during his stay in Yucatán—possibly in 1951 during his first visit to Lerma—the same period in which he wrote *Mayan Letters*. "Human Universe" is the first explicit elaboration of the "stance towards reality" that he introduced in "Projective Verse." Here Olson touches upon the issues that held his mind throughout his life: a) the *laws of the universe* and *man's place* in it; b) *humanism* as opposed to some *alternative stance;* and c) the problems of language in modern civilizations, especially those related to *the universe of discourse.*

There are laws, Olson begins, and the universe—both the human universe and "that other" one—is there for discovery. The problem is that man has settled for too little knowledge, "happy he at least makes a little sense."[15] Definition follows discovery too quickly. The epistemological problem of humanism is first, that the reflex of *definition* has become as much a part of discovery as *sensation,* and second, that in the limited "human universe" it is hardly possible to escape subjectivity: "The difficulty of discovery (in the close world which the human is because it is ourselves and nothing outside us, like the other) is, that definition is as much part of the act as is sensation itself, in this sense, that life *is* preoccupation with itself, that conjecture about it is as much of it as its coming at us, its going on. In other words, we are ourselves both the instrument of discovery and instrument of definition" (HU, 53).

Man has developed beyond language, "discourse," which attempts to incorporate both definition *and* sensation, having a "double sense of discrimination (logos) and of shout (tongue)" (HU, 53). For one to take a different epistemological route one must first examine language, the vehicle of discourse.

Language, at least since 450 B.C., has been overbalanced/overpowered by *one* element of the dichotomy of logos vs. tongue, discrimination vs. shout. *Logos,* which Olson defined in "Projective Verse" as "word as thought" (PV, 21), has taken over the functions of language: since the time of the great Greeks (Socrates, Aristotle, Plato), generalization, logic and classification, and idealism have all gained power. Man has shut himself *away* from experience, and closed himself into his limited "human universe." Thus *humanism* can be blamed for enclosing all speculation in the "UNIVERSE of discourse" (to which "logos [is] given so much more of its part than live speech"). Olson argues that "discourse has arrogated to itself a good deal of experience" (HU, 54).

Olson blames the Greeks for limiting "our participating in our experience," thereby preventing "discovery." First, he blames Socrates for his "readiness to generalize, his willingness . . . to make a 'universe' out of discourse instead of letting it rest in its most serviceable place" (HU, 54). Next, he blames Aristotle for generating habits of thought based on logic and classification. Third, he blames Plato for preventing knowledge and discovery by emphasizing the superiority of the Ideal over the Real. "Idealism of any sort," Olson declares, "like logic and classification, intervene at just the moment they become more than the means they are, are allowed to become ways as end instead of ways *to* an end" (HU, 55). Put simply, "Any tendency to abstract general statement is a greased slide," as Olson learned from Pound.[16]

The Greeks take logos as the final discipline, Olson insists, and fail to notice that beyond logos and reason there is *direct perception,* and that the harmony of the universe is "post-logical," that is, it cannot be grasped by logic.

The task of man today, therefore, is twofold:

1) He needs to recover the *two* universes man lives in, and to return experience to "the only two universes which count, the two phenomenal ones, the two a man has need to bear on because they bear so on him: that of himself, as organism, and that of his environment, the earth and planets" (HU, 54).

2) In terms of language, "language's other function, speech, seems so in need of restoration" (HU, 54). Logos should be given only as much significance and power as does not prevent and limit discovery and knowing. At the same time, the distinction between logos and shout needs to be balanced: "The distinction here is between language as the act of the instant and language as the act of thought about the instant" (HU, 54).

"It is not the Greeks I blame," Olson goes on (HU, 56). It is an understandable reflex, he explains, that when "we do not find ways to hew to experience" we "stay in the human universe" and thus "partition" reality (HU, 56). Selecting, demonstrating, separating out—they are all juxtaposed to experience and are thus unsatisfactory acts of living and writing (HU, 55). Olson blames *comparison* and *symbology* as "the false faces, too much seen, which hide and keep from use the active intellectual states, metaphor and performance" (HU, 56). Comparison and symbology are as much part of this "universe of discourse" as description is; in fact, they all counterbalance the same values: experience, action, self-existence.

"Representation was never off the dead-spot of description. Nothing was *happening* as of the poem itself. . . . It was referential to reality," "Olson wrote in his letter to Elaine Feinstein (PV, 28). He puts these ideas more sharply in "Human Universe":

All that comparison ever does is set up a series of *reference* points: to compare is to take one thing and try to understand it by marking its similarities to or differences from another thing. Right here is the trouble. . . . such an analysis only accomplishes a *description,* does not come to grips with what really matters: that a thing, any thing, impinges on us by a more important fact, its self-existence, without reference to any other thing. . . . That is what we are confronted by, not the thing's "class," any hierarchy, of quality or quantity, but the thing itself, and its *relevance* to ourselves who are the experience of it. (HU, 56)

Olson is against description, comparison, and symbology because these literary techniques deny the processural nature of reality. An object, an entity, or a phenomenon can only be approached as self-existing and not with reference to other objects. "Each actual entity," as Robert von Hallberg explains Olson's view, "is finally so distinctly itself that it eludes analogical categories. Each thing's process of self-formation is a record of simile and comparison; but . . . it is . . . to describe its process of self-formation rather than its interaction with the subject. At the end of such a description one has only a second-hand thing, the thing filtered through and to some extent, no matter how precise and apt the simile and comparison, distorted by language."[17] Olson would agree: analytical categories like description, comparison, and simile are secondhand things, incapable of grasping the process and self-formation of the things in question. They filter and distort sensory experience. In trying to set up an "alternative to the whole Greek system" (HU, 55), he is looking for "a way which bears *in* instead of away, which meets head on what goes on each split second, a way which does not—in order to define—prevent, deter, distract and so cease the act of, discovering" (HU, 56).

In Lerma, Mexico, he seems to have found all the primeval values that Western humanism has lost. Although "poor failures of the modern world," the descendants of Maya civilization "do one thing no modern knows the secret of, he is still by nature possessed of it: they wear their flesh with that difference which the understanding that it is common leads to" (HU, 57). Their natural law of flesh, Olson explains, is not that "pull-away" that one would find in America, but *touch,* a direct admission and obedience to the "wild reachings of his organism" and their acceptance of themselves as "curious wandering animals" with attentive "animal human eyes" (HU, 57).

The Maya, Olson proceeded to explain, were capable of unusual civilizational and cultural achievements exactly because they "were able to stay so interested in the expression and gesture of all creatures, including at least three planets in addition to the human face, eyes and hands" (HU, 58). Among their achievements Olson listed: the invention of a system of written record, the hieroglyphs, which could "retain the power of the objects of which they are the images; the building of huge firetowers and observatories out of stone; and fired clay pots. On top of all this, they were capable of making "an improvement on nature—the domestication of maize—which remains one of the world's wonders" (58). For Olson, however, the most amazing feature of these people, one that is detectable even in their descendants, was their *posture,* in harmony with their "management of external nature": "They still carry their bodies with some of the savor and the flavor that the bodies of the Americans are as missing in as their irrigated lettuce and their green-picked refrigerator ripened fruit" (HU, 58). Olson's judgment on America and the Western world for wanting nothing but the same old thing was harsh indeed: "Spectatorism crowds out participation as the condition of culture. . . . All individual energy and ingenuity is bought off. . . . Passivity conquers all. Even war and peace die . . . and man reverts to only two of his components, inertia and gas. . . . Value is perishing from the earth because no one cares to fight down to it beneath the glowing surfaces so attractive to all. Der Weg stirbt" (HU, 58–59).

Part 2   In the second part of the essay Olson tries to find ways to fight inertia, lack of individual energy, and passivity, and to show *the way* (Der Weg) that might help man "repossess him of his dynamic" (HU, 59). Inherited Judeo-Christian formulations, for example, "the notion of himself as the center of phenomenon by fiat or of god as the center and man as god's chief reflection," are destructive. A worldview based on either god or man as the center of all things sets aside nature. The process has to be turned back. Man must realize nature is "the most powerful agent of all," that nature had to be given its place, "but without somehow, remembering what truth there was in man's centering the use of anything . . . in himself" (HU, 59).

Instead of false distinction based on the dichotomy of *chaos* and *order,* Olson proposed the dichotomy of *"unselectedness"* as "man's original condition" and *"selectiveness"* as the original "impulse by which he proceeds to do something about the unselectedness" (HU, 59–60). Olson's act of *selection* is centered around the *senses,* which he elevated to the highest intellectual level. He did not even mention in this part the "ordering faculties" of generalization, logic and classification, and idealism—the pillars of the Western humanistic tradition that have helped to destroy man. He goes on to insist that the "fingertips" (perception, sensation, reception) are man's "little brains" (responding to external stimuli and making decisions), or, in the traditional formula, his soul: "By making the threshold of reception so important and by putting the instrumentation of selection so far out from its traditional place (the greatest humanist of them all opened a sonnet, 'Poor soul, the centre of my sinful earth'), you have gone so far as to imply that the skin itself, the meeting edge of man and external reality, is where all that matters does happen, that man and external reality are so involved with one another that, for man's purposes, they had better be taken as one." (HU, 60).

Olson was willing to go so far and to commit the "crime" of taking man and external reality as *one* from the point of view of the skin. In this way Olson hopes "to restore to man some of his lost relevance."

But Olson uses the metaphor of the senses ("of the literal speed of light by which a man absorbs, instant on instant, all that phenomenon presents him") as an image "of the ways of his inner energy, of the ways of those other things which are usually, for some reason, separated from the external pick-ups—his dreams, for example, his thoughts . . . , his desires, sins, hopes, fears, faiths, loves" (HU, 60). He refuses to believe that "these so-called inner things are so separable from objects, persons, events which are the content of them" (HU, 60).

Man's personality is built upon the way his senses select from the phenomenal field. This selection, this process of individuation, is not, Olson insistently argued, peculiar to man. Selection depends upon the organism, the senses, and not the soul. Neither is that "process by which man transposes phenomenon to his use," he goes on, "any more extricable from reception than reception itself is from content" (HU, 61).

Thus, only one kind of relation to reality is valid: reception of and participation in the process of selection from phenomenon, and its transposition to one's own "use." Description and definition are, on the other hand, not valid, Olson claims: even scientific measurement is impossible, he points out, citing nuclear physicist Werner Heisenberg, who "had the intelligence to admit in his principle that a thing can be measured in its mass only by arbitrarily assuming a stopping of its motion" (HU, 61). In other words, only the artistic/poetic relation is valid: comprehending the process, "by way of the skin," and enacting it, "out again." Such poetry will be a "tremendous discharge of force" (HU, 62): "it is the equal of its cause only when it proceeds unbroken from the threshold of a man through him and back out again, without loss of quality, to the external world from which it came. . . . The meeting edge of man and the world is also his cutting edge. If man is active, it is exactly here where experience comes in that it is delivered back, and if he stays fresh at the coming in he will be fresh at his going out" (HU, 62).

Olson referred to Rimbaud and the hieroglyphs of the Maya as examples of cultural achievements that use aural energies without loss, which do not depart from nature but are proofs of it. He also pointed to scholars who "explain" history and literature as people who arrest and divert the force of nature, who diminish its energy. They cannot do anything else, since they "know nothing in not knowing how to reify what they do know. . . . they do not know how to pass over to us the energy implicit in any high work of the past because they purposely destroy that energy" (HU, 63). Modern man, Olson goes on, destroys energy every day: "Man has made himself an ugliness and a bore" (HU, 64).

Olson found a great lesson in Mayan civilization. "We should discover," as one of my students pointed out in her term paper on "Human Universe," "in fact, realize, the importance of the things the Maya instinctively know. It is not that we should be 'curious wandering animals' and do away with our civilization, but that we must know we are not more than curious wandering animals even with our civilization."

Olson concluded with a Mayan story about the romance of sun and moon. The story presents these planets, birds and other earthly animals, plants, and man as comparable, or, what is more, equal, parts of the phenomenal world. Unlike many stories of origin and creation, this one has none of the dualism of humanistic metaphysics; the natural world is not there to explain the human world. Instead, all create *one* universe, the universe or organisms *and* planets, where motion from the world of plants and insects to the world of rivers and planets is smooth and natural, hardly noticeable. This, the big one, is our true "human universe."

Several lessons can be drawn from the essay "Human Universe." The first concerns Olson's elevation of the senses ("fingertips") to the level of "little brains," or soul, which should be the main faculty of *creativity*. "[I]t is the nature of perception, of attention," Olson insistently claims, that it is "a spiritual condition." Attention or perception, the "sharp sure hunger of the senses," when it is a condition of *intensity,* is a spiritual condition. Today the greatest danger to life is the lack of the intensive spiritual condition, slackness, laziness, limpness (*Muthologos,* 2:170). The poet who demands attention in intellectual spheres must be the most attentive person in seemingly minor matters of everyday life, too. Charles Boer recounts how sensitive Olson was to landscapes, notes that he was the only person who cared enough to remember all the names of the numerous Moynihan children, relates that he felt an increasing resistance toward casual socializing, stating that "I don't socialize, I personalize" (Boer, 102, 48, 96). "The diversity of his attention," Christensen aptly puts it, was "almost a greed for experience" (Christensen, 7).

Attention implies involvement, the engagement with things one considers necessary, with a community and place, attention to the whole context we live in. "Polis is / eyes," Olson writes in "Letter 6" of *Maximus.*

Attention is the process through which the boundary between subject and object is dissolved. It helps to achieve a "pure, utterly marvelous divine existence," Olson remarked. Attention creates a spiritual state in which "the experience outside is definitely identical with the experience inside" (*Muthologos,* 1:60). Attention, as he said plainly in the same talk, "as a mobile fact constantly is re-mobilizing the object that sets itself in motion"; as such, it is "the source of our very existence as human beings" (*Muthologos,* 1:58, 59).

Attention is the primary agent of creativity for Olson. In "Human Universe" he elaborated the way "coming in" and "going out" are *one* process. Because art is the only "twin" of life, only art can create or re-create (give back) nature's forces without loss of energy. Actually, as Merrill points out, Olson uses a term he borrowed from cybernetics, *feedback,* as a law to define the nature of the creative process. He read about feedback in Norbert Wiener's books. Writing or painting or composing music can be a twin of life because it right away *feeds back,* without entering another phase, without halting the process. Poems born out of such constantly moving creative processes do not lose energy and force; all that is "in front of the senses" in moments of intensive awareness and perception are part of the "going out" (Merrill, 78).

Olson is interested in the nature of feedback as an epistemological term. As Merrill explains, for Olson feedback is "the technique man employs for obedience to 'nature's force.' In a universe of process, of incessant change, man must assume a posture that will tap rather than obstruct the inherent energy of that change. . . . The law of feedback is the most demonstrable in man's creative acts" (Merrill, 78–79). *Communication,* whether artistic communication or everyday conversation, is the way man feeds back to external reality. Merrill defines the law of Olson's art as the law of feedback: "His art, as it 'twins' reality, must keep moving abreast with what is going on, forging ahead in a circular envelopment of the subject, never emending, never changing, but, true to the process of his activity, keeping up with the moment and 'feeding back' what comes at him fresh at the threshold of the skin" (80).

Apart from Olson's link to Norbert Wiener, one other intellectual tie needs to be mentioned in connection with Olson's theory of attention: gestalt therapy. Paul Goodman, writer, philosopher, and pedagogue, provided this link for Olson at Black Mountain. Goodman was, as Paul Christensen points out, "Olson's counterpart in educational theory and social thought." Goodman argued that perception was "a complex process involving memory, emotion and bodily sensation, as well as intellection, and when any of these sources of input is repressed there is a proportional diminution of excitement, and the self begins to atrophy" (Christensen, 29–30).

In Goodman's line of gestalt thinking we find the same elements and concepts as in Olson's version of perception theory: participation, attention, perception, individuation. "[T]hrough the full participation of the organism with the field of its environment," as Christensen paraphrases Goodman, "the self is created" (31).

The concept of *obedience* is inseparable from Olson's feedback notion and his elevation of sensuality. Among all the articulations of obedience, one feature is constant: Olson's blind faith in what he once called the "life in us." This obedient stance implies a holding back of ego-consciousness, not in the sense of Eliot's impersonality in seeking to suppress the opinions and judgments of the individual, but in the sense of not adulterating with the individual's thoughts the selection and accumulation of knowledge gained by the five senses.

The epistemological posture Olson elaborates in "Human Universe" provides the outline of Olson's alternative to humanism. In his philosophical system marked by signposts such as attention, objectism, humility, and obedience, Olson cuts man down to his proper size and indicates his proper mission. Olson sees man as one object among multitudes, forces, and dimensions larger than himself, who must learn to live in correspondence with the world around him. The natural consequence of learning this lesson will be increased activity and creativity. Robert von Hallberg correctly emphasizes Olson's desire to achieve a "human universe where man exists feelingly in the same space and time with the objects of his perception" (von Hallberg 1974, 91).

The ethical imperative of "Human Universe" is unlike that the Objectivists proclaim (despite many resemblances stemming from a shared zeitgeist). Olson affirms humanity by insisting that "making is more valuable than what is made, because only by activity is man fully human" (von Hallberg 1974, 92). This is Olson's new humanism.

Chapter Three

Projectivism in Practice: Olson's Epistemology and Concept of Language

Olson's poetic achievement culminated in the elaboration of a poetic language that was designed to contain his universe without restrictions. He developed this language, necessitated by his projectivist stance, as a response to the controlling grip of Western "literacy."

The essays "Projective Verse" and "Human Universe" seem to be, in Merrill's term, the "literary tip of a metaphysical iceberg" (48). They contain Olson's *ars poetica* grounded in a strong philosophical-metaphysical system. This metaphysical foundation is not unique, for other poets and writers of the 1950s and 1960s shared some or all of Olson's assumptions. But, then, Olson himself liked to cite the Hungarian mathematician Farkas Bolyai, who said: "Each idea has, so to say, its own epoch when it is discovered in different places at the same time, just as in spring the violets sprout wherever the sun shines."[1]

"We belong to a community," in the words of Werner Heisenberg, "kept together by common ideas, by a common scale of ethical values, or by a common language in which one speaks about the general problems of life."[2] Our community, in Olson's interpretation, is not simply made up of the violets, but also of those who are sensitive to their smell: "It is still something, the fragrance, that only those with/ the nose for it can smell and/CAN GIVE OFF" ("The Story of an Olson, and Bad Thing").

Against the Western Humanistic Tradition

> We have come full circle. . . .
> Full circle: an end to romans, hippocrats and christians.
> ("The K")

There is an insistent *proposition* (in Whitehead's sense, "lure for feeling") in Olson's poems and essays, lectures and conversations, letters and notes: we have come to the end of a great historical cycle whose monocultural dominant has been the Platonic-Aristotelian tradition. This Western humanistic tradition, and more specifically its discourse, the prison of Hellenism, has kept man away from direct experience, preventing his engagement with the world.

> And words, words, words
> all over everything
> No eyes or ears left
> to do their own doings (all
> invaded, appropriated, outraged, all senses
> including the mind . . .
> ("The Songs of Maximus," Song 1)

During a conversation recorded in 1963, for example, Olson recalled the way he stopped reading to an audience of "nonlisteners" at Brandeis: "You people are so literate," he burst out, "I don't want to read to you anymore." The key word or concept here is "literate," which he explains as follows: "Yes, better to be, really, illiterate. In fact it's very crucial today in these areas to be sure that you stay illiterate simply because literacy is wholly dangerous, so dangerous that I'm involved, every time I read poetry, in the fact that I'm reading to people who are literate—and they are *not* hearing. They may be listening with all their minds, but they don't hear" (*Muthologos,* 1:54).

But this is only one of Olson's many outbursts against the Western humanistic tradition, against "literacy." His insistence that "illiteracy" and projectivism should be used to break down the walls of Hellenistic "literacy" (reason, logic, classification, generalization, mechanical systematization, allegory, symbology, etc.) proved to be one of the most recurrent and dominant ideas permeating Olson's work, perhaps *the* major philosophical ramification of his poetics—one that he supported not only with poetic, literary, and linguistic evidence, but also with philosophical, historical, and scientific evidence. Logic, classification, and symbology are, he insisted, all tools of a cultural tradition that man must "unlearn" so that he may reenter the world.

Merrill cites the poem "La Torre" as one of the many pieces of Olson's writing that attack literacy:

> The tower is broken, the house
> where the head was used to lift,
> where awe was
> And the hands
> (It is broken!
>
> .   .   .   .

>   The end of something has a satisfaction.
>   When the structures go, light
>   comes through

> To begin again. Lightning
> is an axe, transfer
> of force subject to object is
> order: destroy!

As Merrill unfolds and opens up the metaphor of the tower, we realize
that indeed the tower that the poem impels us to destroy is the prison
of Greek epistemology. This epistemological system elevates man's
rational and creative powers (head and hands), and treats them as
superior faculties literally towering above all other faculties. But Olson
sees that the tower, by its gestures of fencing off, delineating, and
rising up high, expresses man's habit of standing apart from and above
nature. "By virtue of these superior attributes," Merrill points out, man
"manipulates nature for his purposes and exiles himself from Her. His
tower is testament to his denial that he is a 'thing among things.' It is
Hellenism itself and it effectively dramatizes how Greek tradition has
'estranged us from that with which we are most familiar' " (Merrill,
41). When the tower is destroyed, man's separateness from all that is
most familiar comes to an end.

>   Where there are no walls
>   there are no laws, forms, sounds, odors
>   to grab hold of

> Let the tower fall!
> Where space is born
> man has a beach to ground on

Merrill also points out that the tower is the dramatization of language,
too, of logical discourse, which has to be destroyed in order to gain

reentry into the universe. Instead of the false egotistic devices of reason and creativity that manipulate reality, Olson insists, different tools and materials are needed: "new stone, new tufa, to finish off this rising tower."

Merrill uses the word *particularism* as the unifying concept behind the various elements of Olson's stance toward the tower: the acts of physicality, topos, place, objectism, complementarity, projectivism, continuity, process, motion—they are all associated with the "old tower" of illiteracy, and should be returned to. They will give us a world of "complex simultaneity" in consonance with the universe of experience that Hellenism is incapable of grasping. Only the projective mode can obediently create an energy field in the poem, the only "twin of life," without the restructuring artificial gesture of literacy. "Reason," as Olson discovered in Ammonius, "distributes too much, dissolves and destroys" (Merrill, 85).

Instead of a universe of discourse Olson offers a universe of experience and illiteracy, with elements such as the acts of physicality, topos, place and particularism, objectism, complementarity, projectivism, continuity, process, and motion. In his search for alternatives to humanistic literacy, Olson turned to civilizations anterior to his own, as well as to new scientific thinking that acknowledged "other" forms of space, thus pushing our boundary of understanding toward a wider circumference.

Olson's cosmology discards Western discursive logic that distrusts perception and relies on will, reason, and tradition. These things are too bound to referential theories that lead through preordained imaginative constructs to "despair." Meaning for Olson is not referential, but "that which exists through itself" (*Muthologos,* 1:64); meaning is process and action, emerging through the event.

Knowledge

> Men are so sure they know very many things,
> they don't even know night and day are one
> ("Maximus, to Gloucester, Sunday, July 19")

Olson took a clear stand against abstract knowledge not grounded in experience. He blamed Pound for not *inhabiting* his own experience, for living a literary life only (Seelye, 99). He blamed today's professors for not being in full possession of their knowledge: "they don't believe what they know" (Boer, 13). He was the one who had studied Melville on the spot, who had gone to Mexico in search of the Maya ("went / looking for a place where people are still natives, and where human / business is still the business," as he wrote in "The Story of an Olson, and Bad Thing") because he had an inner need to discover knowledge via experience. He stressed the importance of "Finding out for oneself," to possess a compassionate understanding of the world. Olson's was, in this sense, the objectivist position which Alfred North Whitehead described as follows: "that the actual elements perceived by our sense are *in themselves* the elements of a common world; and that this world is a complex of things, including indeed our acts of cognition, but transcending them. . . . the things experienced are to be distinguished from our knowledge of them. . . . But the point is that the actual things experienced enter into a common world which transcends knowledge, though it includes knowledge."[3]

By means of this kind of knowledge, this compassionate understanding, the boundary between subject and object dissolves. Olson points out that "attention as a mobile fact constantly is re-mobilizing the object that sets itself in motion," and brings about, as Olson quotes that "beautiful concept" of Whitehead, "the knowledge-bringing event," "the eternal event that strikes across all object and occasion" (*Muthologos,* 1:58, 59). Attention, "the source of our very existence as human beings," makes subject and the world coincide: "only if there is a coincidence of yourself/& the universe is there then in fact/an event" (from "The Lamp"). Life only happens when one is interested, concerned, open to experience, in a condition of alertness. "You can be in the middle of even an explosion," Duncan explains in a dialogue on history with Olson, "if you're not interested, it isn't happening. . . . It's simply a matter of being concerned with the event that's there" (*Muthologos,* 1:8–9). In other words, only concern, attention, interest, a turning toward the world can make life happen, or bring about events. And the world lying around us can only be known and understood compassionately, through this attentive concern. Olson liked to quote Whitehead's "enormous statement" (*Muthologos,* 1:50): "All is there for feeling." Or I can cite his own: "polis is / eyes."

> Eyes
> & polis,
> fishermen
> & poets

or in every human head I've known is
busy
both:
the attention, and
the care
however much each of us
chooses our own
kin and
concentration

. . . .

so few
have the polis
in their eye

(from "Letter 6")

The poem for Olson can only happen, be an event, if it stems from such compassionate knowledge, from attention and perception. D. H. Lawrence calls it the visionary image, the capacity to "see the divine in natural objects."[4]

The poetic imagination is closely linked with conditions of ordinary experience, and thus articulates acts of attention. An act of attention exhibits, in Whitehead's words, "a direct joy in the apprehension of the things which lie around us" (Whitehead, 19–20). And because such apprehension is "the source of our very existence as human beings," the determining characteristic of the poet will be his greater-than-usual ability to be attentive: "[A] creative man is, 1st, an alive one, and, as alive, takes care of his business, including his skills," Olson wrote to Cid Corman. Art to be found at the "cutting edge": "the wedge of the WHOLE FRONT."[5]

Objective Reality

Apprehension, however, is not simply the source of *our* existence as human beings: it is also the source of existence of the world that we inhabit. "To look at it is more / than it was," writes Creeley. This idea is not unique to Olson: modern nuclear science, as Olson knew quite well, has also questioned the existence of a so-called objective reality independent of observation. In classical physics only, the brilliant physicist Heisenberg claims, "one was led to the tacit assumption that there existed an objective course of events in space and time, independent of

observation; further, that space and time were categories of classification of all events, . . . and thus represented an objective reality, which
was the same to all men."[6] This basic assumption of classical physics
was first undermined by Einstein, through his special theory of relativity; eventually the concepts of objective space and time were proved
wrong by experimental investigations. The "objective" world was an
illusion, a "product of our active intervention, and improved technique
of observation" (Heisenberg, 70).

The "wonderful method" of uncertainty relations has entered the
study of natural phenomena; moreover, the dividing line between observation and the observed object has proved "immaterial." "Modern physics," Heisenberg declares, "has taught us to do without an absolute
scale of time and of objective events in space and time" (17). The
introduction of concepts of *potentiality* and indeterminacy into physical
science led to a major change in the physicists' epistemological theory:
the atoms or the elementary particles "form a world of potentialities or
possibilities rather than one of things or facts" (Heisenberg, 1958,
160).

From this scientific thinking Olson learned to question the division
between subject and object. Both scientist and poet can have no idea of
the form of existence of an objective world independent of observation:
we are necessarily always part of what we see. Our very seeing—our
acts of perception, attention, concern, intensive presence, understanding, response—re-creates and possibly transforms what we see.

Mystery of the Unknown

The replacement of the classical concept of an objective reality with
uncertainty and indeterminacy changed the epistemological stance of
modern physics and eventually that of modern poetry as well. For
Olson, poetry shall be drawn to what is not known, to the mystery of
being, without the compulsion to *solve* the mystery. "[M]ost life is,"
Olson said, "literally the understanding that you don't understand"
(*Muthologos,* 1:173). The poet, as Heisenberg suggests, like Columbus
leaving the known world, is drawn to the unknown: he seems to obey
some direction, he seems to intuit that writing is something given him
to do. Writing is a discovery, made in obedient acceptance of whatever
agency there is beside the writer. His is an obedience to a presence that
is not ever understood, an obedience so strong that it finds joy in not
understanding.

"Stance towards reality"—"Contrary-Renaissance"

Olson's stance toward reality came together from various sources: from modern philosophy, nuclear physics, non-Euclidean geometries, Eastern religions, primitive civilizations—all that, taken together, produced what he calls a "contrary-Renaissance."

This contrary-Renaissance, Olson claims, began to evolve sometime around the middle of the nineteenth century, with the creation of non-Euclidean geometries by Bolyai, Lobatchevsky, and Riemann. Non-Euclidean geometry insists that space is not something independent of objects and masses that are situated within it, but is determined by those very bodies. The parameters that characterize space are not constant, but vary from point to point depending, among other things, on the mass distribution of matter filling space. "Some forces of nature obey one, and some of them the other, from our point of view specific, geometry," Lobatchevsky wrote.[7] Twentieth-century science and philosophy supported non-Euclidean geometry in several ways: with Einstein's theory of relativity, with the concept of the electromagnetic field in which velocity and force and not the inert particles are parameters, with Whitehead's philosophy of a continuous world characterized not by discrete entities but by process and change, with the notion of a continuous universe, where time is the fourth dimension, where substances turn into events and qualities into quantities. Olson's aesthetic theory developed on such foundations of scientific and philosophic thinking, and proposed a new kind of writing using these scientific discoveries as well as Whiteheadian philosophy (to which Olson was already committed before he read Whitehead's books and made his acquaintance).

Against Discourse

"My father was old fashion. . . . He was scrupulous about a letter. He had the idea it was somehow important just because it was made up of words (he had the notion that words have value, as signs of meaning and feeling) and because it was a communication between two persons" (*Post Office,* 47). This is how Olson explains his letter-carrier father's awareness of the written and spoken word and the background of his own belief that words have value. Later, in a letter to Dahlberg, Olson went as far as this Pound-like outburst: "To use words wrongly creates evil in the soul" (*LDO,* 1:157). Like the first generation of the moderns, Olson always insisted on precision. His editing instructions had to be taken absolutely seriously; he demanded that the printer obey all his minute spacings and graphics.[8]

He insisted that *Maximus* be spaced with the consciousness of a musical score and had to be set by the printer precisely as directed (because the experience was not just the *language* but the spacings and graphics). Nothing was left to chance. From Dahlberg he learned to appreciate those poets "who try as best they can to call AA, a chair a chair, an alley an alley" (*LDO,* 3:192).

Olson was indeed a poet who took language seriously. He often took detours in his poems to contemplate certain words and phrases, as the following example indicates:

> in the l'univers concentrationnaire the flesh
> (is it not extraordinary that, when a wound
> is healing, we call, what it throws off, proud
> flesh?) flesh, rose flesh
> ("The Story of an Olson, and Bad Thing")

He never gave up the ideal of precision and explicitness. "As a matter of fact, it is actually getting clear to me that the only thing to do that is interesting today is to be explicit," he said in an interview in 1968 (*Muthologos,* 2:102). "Let those who use words cheap, who use us cheap / take themselves out of the way / Let them not talk of what is good for the city" ("Letter 3"). This refusal to "use words cheap" is one of the defining characteristics of Olson's poetry. Of course, poets have always wanted to be precise and to find "the exact word." But Olson not only seeks precise words: in the act of writing, he actually shows us the intellectual process of seeking and finding. The hesitances so typical of Olson arise exactly from this urge to be precise, to reach down into his soul to discover *claritas.* He is constantly adjusting, constantly refining his choice of words.

> that men killed, do kill, that woman kills
> is part, too, of his question
> 2
> That it is simple, what the difference is—
> that a man, men, are now their own wood
> and thus their own hell and paradise
> that they are, in hell or in happiness, merely
> something to be wrought, to be shaped, to be carved, for use, for
> others

does not in the least lessen his, this unhappy man's
obscurities, his
confrontations

("In Cold Hell, in Thicket")

We recognize a constant "precisioning" of language here, an obsession to find the right word, and never to be vague or misleading.

Says Iamblichus:
by shipreck, he perished (Hippasus, that is)
the first to publish (write down, divulge)
the secret,
the construction of, from 12 pentagons,
the sphere

("The Praises," part 3)

In the same poem he explicitly insists on linguistic hygiene: "Avert, avert, avoid/pollution, to be clean/in a dirty time."

A belief in the value of words and in the importance of communication between two persons, a refusal to employ words in a casual and careless manner, a demand for precision and explicitness—these are the features that characterize Olson's stance toward language. Very much like Whitman a century earlier, Olson, too, went on "field trips" into the streets, to bars and truckstops, to overhear and learn from the muscular vernacular of everyday speech. Fielding Dawson remembers how "in commuting from D.C. he and Connie stopped at truckstops for coffee, and listened as he loved to do, to the drivers, Connie smiled, eager in their recent memory, enjoyed his pleasure—'Those guys!' he breathed" (Dawson, 131).

Language, Olson believed, has been corrupted by referentiality, by Hellenism that limits its horizons to rational discourse, by the process of allegorization. The rational, "the will and culture," Olson stated in *The Special View of History,* "was always ready to put out the light. . . . the rational mind hates the familiar, and has to make it ordinary by explaining it, in order not to experience it" (31). Rational discourse *can* put out the light, abstract language or philosophical discourse is incapable of discovering the laws of experience, because they are the product of Western civilization that has cut itself off from direct experience and compassionate understanding of this direct experience: "Power and the abstract/distract a man/from his own gain" ("A Lion upon the Floor").

As part of his language purification program, he warns us against using abstract nouns and verbs, signifiers that have no concrete reference in physical reality: "There may be no more names than there are objects/There can be no more verbs than there are actions" ("Tyrian Businesses," 1:5)

Olson gives a critique of discourse, and points to ways in which the damage and loss caused by discourse, such as abstract categorization and generalization, can be mended by a natural language that will restore the dignity of speech and the wholeness of the human self. Western Aristotelian thinking imposes its hierarchical model of classification and logic upon cognition, and thus makes it a rigid and closed system. Olson does not believe in the validity of ideas prior to experience, by which order is imposed upon the world, and does believe that the poem born out of this kind of cognition is nothing more than a product of discourse. Such a poem represents a spiritual estrangement from the laws of creation because it is imposed upon reality instead of being part of it.

"Universe of discourse" and "universe of experience" are the terms that best describe Olson's theory of language. The former is bad, because discourse, in Merrill's words, surrenders "the fullness of experience for the sake of logical tidiness" (38). The latter is good because it results in language used in a projective way to reenact experience. Olson opposes discourse that is representational, mimetic, and referential to reality to a language, shout, or tongue that is part of reality. One is *about* experience, the other is *of* it. Talk or speech is spontaneous, processural, and conversational, that is, it is full of inconsistencies and uncertainties. This language based on the projective act adheres to the flow of events; discourse, on the other hand, ignores the continuum of events by making artificial jumps using allegories, symbols, and comparisons.

The hierarchical model of logic and classification imposed upon cognition has created a discourse that has resulted in man's spiritual estrangement from that "which is most familiar." Language has made of itself a tower of separateness alienated from experience. The complete sentence is an integral part of the discourse that Olson wants to destroy with the tower of Hellenism. He rejects the artificiality of the sentence as a "complete thought"; a sentence is counter to the striving of nature where process and continuity—but never finality and completeness— are the ideal virtues. This line of thinking reminds me of Robert Duncan saying in a private conversation that the word *sentence* still has for him the Biblical meaning of the "imposition of judgment," words with "strong performative power"—the kind of force and power that discourse has lost forever in the service of reason.

Olson's Language of Illiteracy—Immanence

Olson, in consonance with several other modernists, was engaged in creating a language that was not referential, mimetic, and interpretive of reality, but instead actually part of reality, that is, made up of words that had the solidity of objects—speech that became action, and poetry that was a field of action, field of forces, field of events. Language, as part of reality, Olson's line of thinking goes, shares with reality the laws immanent in nature in that language has laws similar to nature. The "laws of creation" permeate language as well as nature, he insisted. These are not man-made laws—man's task is only to explore them (and not impose them). The poet must approach language with humility (instead of trying to master it), he must be open, emptied out; he must listen to language, and be governed by a trust in the discovery of innate form.

This is the linguistic aspect of the immanentist theory. The poet who attempts to master language and, through discourse, cognition, will, if he imposes his form (and those he inherited from Western Hellenistic tradition), have no access to experience. He will end up with a skeleton of language limited by human control, and poetry that fails to reveal immanent values and meanings. But the poet who approaches language openly, accepting the idea that he is as much object as agent of creativity, that is, if his manner of using language extends beyond the normative rules that impose an external, artificial Aristotelian order upon language, language will reveal its immanent meanings as it reenacts reality.

There are several ways to allow the immanent meanings of language to be revealed. Spring will come, life will be revealed when, as Olson put it in "Projective Verse," "*all* parts of speech suddenly, in composition by field, are fresh for both sound and percussive use, spring up like unknown, unnamed vegetables in the patch, when you work with it" (PV, 21).

1. *Etymology,* for example, is a storehouse of meanings. Each word carries a whole history of meanings but these layers of meanings are ignored or constricted by the poet who tries to impose form on his work. The interaction of latent etymological meanings is a signature of Olson's best poems. ("Root person in root place," he writes in "Letter

3.") He was aware of the roots of nouns, roots that contain cosmic connections: "It is the radical, the root, he and I," he writes in "La Préface," a poem rich in inferences related to Olson's use of Latin root words—*via, vita nuova, apex, pyramid, cunnus*—as well as words of his own coining (out of roots): *deathhead* (apex of the pyramid, of dead bodies in Buchenwald), *polytopes* (stock rhetorical theme, topic).

2. *Morphology* and *sound structure* provide a wealth of immanent meanings for those who take language seriously. Olson recognized that the meaningful or not meaningful segmentation of words and sound clusters could be used to invoke associations with other words and sounds to multiply the semantic possibilities that resonate in a poem. For example, *convert/invert* ("In Cold Hell, in Thicket"); *mu-sick* ("ABC's, 3," "letter 3," "I, Maximus of Gloucester, to You") ("the trick / of corporations, newspapers, slick magazines, movie houses, / the ships, even the wharves, absentee-owned," "Letter 3"); *pick-nicks* ("Letter 6"); *po-ets* ("Maximus, to Gloucester"); *dum-dummed* ("Adamo Me").

Olson loved to coin words: *pejorocracy* ("I, Maximus of Gloucester, to You"); *borning* (active form of "being born," in "The Story of an Olson, and Bad Thing"); *musickracket* (clattering noise, social whirl, fraudulent scheme—here taking on the featurs of *mu-sick:* corruption, ownership, bribery, intimidation—"The Songs of Maximus," Song 3). He also liked to employ little-used or archaic words: *vainglorious* ("Some Good News"); *remonstrance* (representation, demonstration; stating points of opposition or grievance—here in interference with *remembrance*—"Adamo Me").

Olson's idiosyncrasies of spelling were employed intentionally to bring out the tactile/concrete/solid nature of words. Olson used spelling to alert us to the actual taste of words in the mouth: *spiritchool* (spiritual, "The Story of an Olson, and Bad Thing"); *antsirs* (answers, "The Story of an Olson, and Bad Thing"); *biz-i-ness* (business, "The Story of an Olson, and Bad Thing"); *chuman, hoomin* (human, "Issue, Mood"); *so-fist-ik-kashun* (sophistication, "Issue, Mood"); *sirrah* (sorry, "Issue, Mood"); *abt, yr, cld, wd* (common in notes, letters).

3. *Semantics,* or the *meaning of words,* offers various possibilities for the postmodern poet. Uncertainty about the true meaning of many words is pervasive. In an autonomous way, words seem to live their own semantic lives independent of the user (*musickracket, pick-nicks, borning, pejorocracy*). Heisenberg talks about an "intrinsic uncertainty of the meaning of words" (Heisenberg 1958, 146), and this same assumption

lies at the root of Olson's poetics that proclaims responsiveness as the major component of writing. Olson taught that the ability to respond to language, obey it, and accept the permission of language to enter its own world, were basic virtues of writing. From his immanentist stance, Olson strived to liberate language from man-made laws by responding to and trying to hear what immanent order language itself is suggesting to the poet.

Olson discovered rich possibilities by violating subcategorization rules of parts of speech: *an olson* ("The Story of an Olson, and Bad Thing"); *borning* ("The Story of an Olson, and Bad Thing"); *the christ* ("Adamo Me"); *horror his* (as verb, "La Préface"); *I intent upon idlers* (as verb, "Merce of Egypt"); *she chose the ugliest to bed with* (as verb—exists but is archaic—"The Ring of").

When approached in this way, language lifts the barrier of rationality, and the poet is permitted entry into the inner circles and immanent order of language. Once in this sphere, he does not strive to achieve understanding; his acts of overhearing and intimating replace the need for rational comprehension and understanding.

Olson's handling of semantics and his reliance on etymology point in one direction: to linguistic *concretism*. Olson insisted on treating language concretely, on treating words as solid objects with a tactile quality. Olson believed that *foreign words,* where the meaning is not evoked by the sound structure, create this tactile quality most directly: *l'univers concentrationnaire, amour propre* ("The Story of an Olson, and Bad Thing"); *de bacalaos,* / "On ne doit aux morts nothing / else than / la vérité" ("On First Looking Out through Juan de la Cosa's Eyes"). *Puns,* in this context, gain added significance: *via/vita* ("La Préface"); *reverend/reverse* ("ABC's"); *the dyes / of realism* ("ABC's 3"); *oilskins/Olsen* ("Letter 6").

Charles Stein deals at length with Olson's technique of punning. "The treatment of words as solids allows the pun to have its play," he explains; "word which sound alike, are alike, in that they occupy an adjacent or overlapping psychic topography."[9] Stein lists several instances of punning. In "Maximus, from Dogtown—II," the dense punning (*J-son; Hines/sight; Ol'/son*) reveals the poet's hidden conviction about his spiritual ancestry in the second millenium B.C., as well as the themes of backward vision and of identity of father and son. In several Maximus poems, Stein goes on, place-name rhymes suggest possible archetypal connections (*Dog—Dogtown; Mt. Cassius—Cashes*); "the

place-name," Stein suggests, "becomes a site for the projection of 'archetypal force' " (52).

The essay *Casual Mythology* is another example: it is organized around
the punning relationship between two Latin words: *Urbs* (city; Gr. *polis*)
and *Orb* (sphere; earth as globe). "[T]he controlling theme of this
lecture is," Stein explains, "that the 'Imago Mundi' . . . is now capable
of projection onto the earth in such a way that the entire earth (orb)
appears as a single city (urbs)" (Stein, 52). Permitting linguistic coincidence to guide his line of thinking is, I think, a basic characteristic of
Olson's stance; language can be trusted as an epistemological guideline,
too.

Olson's insistence on the literal, concrete, and tactile quality of
words implies his treatment/conception of language as substance and
material. What Robert Kern writes of Creeley's "interest in language *as
language*" applies precisely to Olson, too: they both refuse to take
language as mimetic and referential to reality by suspending significa-
tion for the sake of concretism. [10]

It is perhaps *syntax* that provides the richest possibilities for immanent meanings to emerge. "All that on syntax," Olson wrote to Vincent
Ferrini, "is due to, this: we have to kick sentences in the face . . .
language has to be found out, anew." [11] Syntax is the greatest source of
energy in language where meaning is not referential but arises from an
interplay of forces. This is what Olson calls the "law of the line": "that
the conventions which logic has forced on syntax must be broken open
as quietly as must the too set feet of the old" (PV, 21).

Butterick posits this "flexibility in syntax" as one of the most important characteristics of postmodern relativist poetics, which is "relational
rather than rational" (Butterick 1984, 134). Here words are permitted
to enter into new combinations with each other without the control of
the complete sentence (which is always redundant in a multiple way);
syntactic connections remain richly open when not restrained by fixed
combination points so that speech may follow jumps of thinking and
not be impeded by syntactic breaks. This liberation results in a multi-
valence of combinations and enables rich but formerly latent meanings
to surface.

Too high a price has been paid for logical tidiness and abstract
knowledge, Olson suggests; man has given up the wholeness of experience, together with the wholeness of language. Paratactic language was
exchanged for the periodic sentence; complete thought took over the

domain of dynamic wholeness, that might well include ambiguities, unclarities, irrationalities, and not-understandings. Artificiality has occupied the territory of naturalness.

Stephen Fredman, in his illuminating book on the development of the sentence in modernist-postmodernist American poetry, states clearly the syntactic distinction between completeness and wholeness: "*Wholeness* and *completeness* represent two modes of order and closure available in a sentence. . . . *wholeness* will represent organic, implicit, or generative forms of the sentence (often employing parataxis), and completeness will represent normative, explicit, or preconceived forms of the sentence (often exhibiting hypotaxis)."[12]

Olson rejects sentences as "complete thoughts" in favor of wholeness, where an ideal of harmony or gestalt is present. Characteristically, Olson liked to leave sentences unfinished, or, more precisely, to finish them in a peculiar way: through a big jump, and then to round out his thought with a new sentence or clause relevant in its own way to the preceding semantic concept.

> go still
> now that your legs
>
> the Charleston
> is still for us
>
> You can watch
> It is too late
> to try to teach us
>
> we are the process
> and our feet
> We do not march
> ("I, Mencius, Pupil of the Master")

These sentences are not "complete" in the grammatical sense, but they are whole; to use Olson's word, they *cohere* ("Letter 3").

In Olson's poetry, Fredman points out, "the act of thinking is graphed in its free movement among various conceptual systems"; the result is a "rapid-fire, speech-generated" text (Fredman, 59, 64). This text seems to have a voice of its own, as if language itself was speaking rapidly, obsessively.

> In cold hell, in thicket, how
> abstract (as high mind, as not lust, as love is) how
> strong (as strut or wing, as polytope, as things are
> constellated) how
> strung, how cold
> can a man stay (can men) confronted
> thus?
> All things are made bitter, words even
> are made to taste like paper, wars get tossed up
> like lead soldiers used to be
> (in a child's attic) lined up
> to be knocked down, as I am,
> by firings from a spit-hardened fort, fronted
> as we are, here, from where we must go
>
> . . . .
>   And who
> can turn this total thing, invert
> and let the ragged sleeves be seen
> by any bitch or common character? Who
> can endure it where it is, where the beasts are met,
> where yourself is, your beloved is, where she
> who is separate from you, is not separate, is not
> goddess, is, as your core is,
> the making of one hell
>
>   where she moves off, where she is
>   no longer arch
>   ("In Cold Hell, in Thicket")

We find a similar rapidity and quickness of language in "The Moon Is the No. 18," where Olson exemplifies the processional nature of his sentence: consecutiveness and contiguity structure these sentences in such a way that the comment/focus of each sentence becomes the topic of the next.

>   . . . while prayers
>   striate the snow, words blow
>   as questions cross fast, fast
>   as flames, as flames form, melt
>   along any darkness

Apposition, the syntactic figure where two adjacent units have the same referent, is a typical syntactic catalyst of linguistic immanence: it is capable of holding several elements alongside one another without subordinating one to the other(s). Several Olson poems are built on appositive structure; in "Variations Done for Gerald Van De Wiele" and "The Cow of Dogtown," for example, the successive layers of thought are deposited, as in coral walls, upon those already present. "The Kingfishers" has a similar appositive structure, with the successive layers being deposited around concepts like the lexicon entry of the bird from the *Encyclopaedia Britannica,* Fernand, Mao, the figure E, Heraclitus and perishability, Whitehead and process, and Wieners and the notion of feedback. In "Letter 6" we find two focal layers, fishermen and poets, in apposition. Illustration, rather than explanation, is the best way to understand Olson's method:

> And the child
> had that name, the arrow of
> as the flight of, the move of
> his mother who adorneth
> ("The Ring Of")

> Yellowstone
> Park of holes
> is death the deceased
> presence on us, the spilling lesion

> of the brilliance
> it is to be alive: to walk onto it
> ("Maximus to Gloucester, Sunday, July 19")

Appositive syntax expresses Olson's conviction about multiplicity and singleness: "we grow up many," he writes in "Maximus, to Himself," "[a]nd the single / is not easily / known."

> Around an appearance, one common model, we grow up
> many. Else how is it,
> if we remain the same,
> we take pleasure now
> in what we did not take pleasure before?
> ("The Kingfishers")

"Singleness," as the poem "Variations Done for Gerald Van De Wiele" testifies, is a precious state of mind; the coincidence of the world and man is a rare gift.

Olson uses *repetition* for two purposes: to provide emphasis and to make his thoughts more clear: "and sound is, is, his / conjecture" ("The Moon Is the Number 18"); "The landscape (the landscape!) again: Gloucester," ("The Librarian"); "but this is (this bone) still (still) no reason /there is none, in this air, there is no reason for / knuckling under, for," ("Adamo Me").

Parenthesis is another device much favored by Olson. It usually serves either to signify an insert into the main text or to indicate something standing in opposition to a previous utterance. Olson tended to use double parenthesis in his earlier poems: in the poem "In Cold Hell, in Thicket," for example, we find neatly separated insertions. "The closed parenthesis reads: the dead bury the dead, / and it is not very interesting," he writes in "La Préface." Often he uses single or no parenthesis, but the inserted alien texts are still recognizable.

> . . . the night
> is blue from the full of the April moon
>
> iris and lilac, birds
> birds, yellow flowers
> white flowers, the Diesel
> does not let up dragging
> the plow
>
> . . . .
>   (O saisons, o chateaux!
> Délires!
>   What soul
> is without fault?
>   ("Variations done for Gerald Van De Wiele")
>
> whatever you have to say, leave
> the roots on, let them
> dangle
> And the dirt
>   just to make clear
>   where they came from
>   ("These Days")

Quotation marks serve the same purpose of separating clusters of words from the text.

In the midst of plenty, walk
as close to
bare
        In the face of sweetness,
piss
        In the time of goodness,
go side, go
smashing, beat them, go as
(as near as you can

tear

In the land of plenty, have
nothing to do with it
        take the way of
the lowest,
including
your legs, go
contrary, go

sing
    ("The Songs of Maximus," song 3)

Because such writing resists completeness and favors intimations of wholeness instead, Olson's text is fragmented, discontinuous, full of disjunctions—thereby physically representing the "undone business" the poet must speak of ("Maximus, to Himself"). The Olson poem is an energy construct charged by conjecture of the reader. Syntax within an Olson poem is typically nontraditional: fixed syntactic connections are abolished, old links disappear so that new linking possibilities can be created.

This unlinking is primarily achieved by the creation of fragmented texts, texts that follow the disjunctions characteristic of intensely hesitant speech: "Who pleas for the heart, for the return of, into the work of, / say, the running of / a street-car?" ("ABC's, 3").

Talk

Only by rejecting the rigid system of discourse can the poet give, in the projective poem, a sensitive transcript of the creative moment. In

this projective mode, the laws of speech, instead of discourse, must be
adhered to. As a consequence, this kind of writing will be conversational: unprepared, improvisational, impromptu—very much like Olson's own obsessive and persistent conversations. It will be full of
jumps, hesitations, stoppings, restarts, hoverings. Conspicuous by its
absence from this kind of writing is completeness and redundancy.

Just as discourse favors redundancy for the sake of reducing ambigu-
ity, speech reacts against redundancy, considering it obsolete and a
waste of intellectual effort. Olson's "An Ode on Nativity" includes the
following lines: "Man's splendor/is a question of which/birth." We all
seem to know how the sentence would close: with words like *informs,
determines, starts out, begins, initiates.* That is, we have various possibilities in our minds, all equally present. But the poem itself reacts against
closure. In the following extract from "The Praises," Olson leaves his
sentence incomplete because it is clear as it is:

>   . . . . Look:
>   to fly? a fly can do that;
>   to try the moon? a moth
>   as well; to walk on water? a straw
>   precedes you

Olson's writing is full of unfinished sentences, as this excerpt from
"The Story of an Olson, and Bad Thing" illustrates:

>   Now all things (in the furnace of fact, all things)
>   (no things in the furnace, in the weather-beaten face of
>   doubt)
>   now all things (including notions, or whatever
>   were once validities,
>   all things now stand
>   (including the likes of you and me, all, all
>
>   must be born out of
>   (God knows you know, Old Goddess, &
>   tremendous Mother)
>   There is birth! there is
>
>   all over the place there is

Olson's sentences will often change directions: he will hesitate, stop
in the middle of a sentence, and then continue in a different direction.

Sometimes his sentences consist of two superimposed, interpolated, syntactic structures:

> la lumière"
> but the kingfisher
> de l'aurore"
> but the kingfisher flew west
> est devant nous!
> he got the color of his breasts
> from the heat of the setting sun!
> ("The Kingfishers")

Olson likes to employ two sentences that are connected at one point. This connecting point will serve different grammatical functions for each sentence, as the following extract from "The Librarian" illustrates

> I saw he was the young musician has been there (been before me)
> before
>
> . . . .
> have I seen it (once
> when my daughter ran
> out on a spit of sand
>
> isn't even there)

Often Olson's sentences are like trains shoved/pushed/rolled into each other:

> I break my father's spine,
>
> the cracks
> I break my mother's back
> are so wide,
> they are not so easily
> Used.
> ("The Pavement")

Logical writing is linear, the projective poem models itself after forms of speech: just as speech follows the jumps of thinking, so the projective poem transcribes the creative moment and attempts to represent it in space. Speech drives the writing on, constantly evading the completing closure, always initiating new beginnings. Indeed, Olson's sen-

tences do not end, but flow into one another, as they do endlessly in the
powerful elegy for his mother:

> Goodbye red moon
> in that color you set
> west of the Cut I should imagine
> forever Mother
>
> After 47 years this month
> a Monday at 9 A.M.
> you set I rise I hope
> a free thing as probably
> what you were Not
> the suffering one you sold
> sowed me on Rise
> Mother from off me
> God damn you God damn me my
> misunderstanding of you
>
> I can die now I just begun to live
> ("Moonset, Gloucester,
> December 1, 1957, 1:58 A.M.")

Whereas the discourse of written language is thinned off by completing
redundancies, with fixed combinational possibilities (they are ab-
sorbed, defined, or cut off), in speech these combinations are left
unlinked. The fewer combination points are neutralized, the richer the
meaning of the text will be.

Event

Olson's language is processural (that is, only a means to an end, and
not also an end in itself). This processural nature of Olson's syntax is
evident in his refusal to write complete sentences and in his use of a
quick language to follow his quick thinking. "Every natural action
obeys by / the straightest possible process," he writes in "The Praises."
The poet's job is to transfer that energy that he possesses or reaches,
without any loss: "that that which has been found out by work may, by
work, be passed on / (without due loss of force) / for use." Since the law
is feedback, energy has to be passed on without restructuring, in its
processural form as it arrived. Language has to follow that "tide in

man" ("The K"), to obey the "life within," to move with lunar forces
beyond human control. This sense of inevitable obedience lies behind
such sentences as the following.

> How shall he who is not happy, who has been so made unclear,
> who is no longer privileged to be at ease, who, in this brush, stands
> reluctant, imageless, unpleasured, caught in a sort of hell, how
> shall he convert this underbrush, how turn this unbidden place
> how trace and arch again
> the necessary goddess?
>
> . . . .
>   And who
>   can turn this total thing, invert
>   and let the ragged sleeves be seen
>   by any bitch or common character? Who
>   can endure it where it is, where the beasts are met,
>   where yourself is, your beloved is, where she
>   who is separate from you, is not separate, is not
>   goddess, is, as your core is,
>   the making of one hell
>   where she moves off, where she is
>   no longer arch
>
>   ("In Cold Hell, in Thicket")

As if these sentences have "gone astray," they seem to be getting far
away from where the sentences set out from at the beginning. As the
poem proceeds, the distance between topic and comment seems to
grow.

Field, Space, Page

Olson refuses to use language as discourse. He believed that language should be an event, an act, a happening. He wanted to allow the
kinetics of language to show forth while testing the chemistry of words.
The page in this context corresponds to the poet's consciousness, to the
"boundary of the self," a place, in Hugh Kenner's words, "where mental clarities occur."[13]

The poem is a field where intensive events may occur without redundancy; but "abundance" (Duncan) and "generosity" (Whitehead) can
only characterize space that is open, kinetic (it derives its energy from
the tension of aperiodic rhythm (Schrödinger), and composed of mate-

rial that—as medium—strives not toward completeness but toward wholeness.

This field of wholeness is well represented in the physicality of the Olson household. Fielding Dawson gives us a minute description of the interior of the 1950 Washington, D.C., house, "that magic puzzle," "Master's handmade little palace," a world populated by paintings by Cagli and Lawrence, Mayan figures from Yucatán, and books marked by greedy consumption.

[I]t was a beautiful, magic little house. . . . Inside the hall a small, dark hallway, wide, dark floorboards, casement windows on the left, beamed ceiling and on the righthand wall framed painting, a labyrinth, by Cagli. . . . White walls, dark wood . . . a chest high bookcase (outside, the tangled front yard). The walls were lined with books among which I browsed, found the edition of *Finnegans Wake* his classmates at Harvard had signed and given him. All in all a scholar's library. . . . Every inch of the place was bewitching . . . the small messy fireplace in the left center wall (to make a five-walled room), on the mantlepiece of which the small, what, 12″ × 16″? watercolor by Lawrence of a naked man, Lawrence, taking a leak in a flower bed. Beside it, in a strewn arrangement where long sticks used in the construction of rifle emplacements Olson had found on the Gettysburg battlefield. And small stone Mayan figures, smuggled out of Yucatan, for he had to have them, and at school when he'd returned, and showed them to us, as he held each figure in hand, and spoke as we watched, all in awe, him more so. . . . And again, notice from my description of the house, maybe a faulty memory, but I recall no desk where he wrote, and I have a nagging thread that says he wrote at the little table in the kitchen. (Dawson, 128–29)

The poetic field corresponds to the broad intellectual space Olson lived in. Christensen sketches an awe-inspiring list:

Olson's enthusiasms encompass such oddments as Hopi language, Maya statuary, non-Euclidean geometry, Melville's fiction, the austere thought structures of Whitehead's philosophy, the fragmentary remains of the Sumerian and Hittite civilizations, Norse, Greek, and Egyptian mythology, numerology and the Tarot, the history of human migration, naval and economic history, the etymology of common words, pre-Socratic philosophy, the historical origins of the New England colonies, the development of the fishing industry off the coast of Massachusetts, accounts of the conquest of Mexico, the collapse of the Aztec and Mayan civilizations. (Christensen, 5–6)

All these interests and enthusiasms were in Olson's "personal possession," not simply the result of detached "reading." Fields of knowledge were, for him, various "languages" to be "read." Only through under-standing these languages does one get a proper knowledge of the past, of history, of mythology, and of the individual. For Olson these inter-ests were deeply related and gave him opportunity to intellectually stretch and expand into the various layers of these cultural units. His expanding intelligence provided the contact between the layers and brought about their fusion into an existing field that we call our climate of opinion. The "magical *mélange* of facts," that, in William Moebius's words, Olson extracted from his diverse interests—ranging from "theoretical physics to Anatolian historiography"—seems to co-here according to laws of projective space as "the magnitudes outside a given gravitational field."[14]

Olson was interested in *the whole,* the orders of the great household; the chopped-up parts did not satisfy him. Frank Davey's remark that Olson was always trying "to toss the universe in your lap" aptly ex-presses this Olsonian characteristic (Merrill, 39). Gestures of bridging, holding the whole simultaneously, expanding, stretching were his. "Put an end to division of all sorts," was his imperative (*Muthologos,* 1:94).

Olson's achievement culminated in the creation of a language that provided the space for this whole. Charged with presence, this space allowed continuously generated relations to emerge both as intellectual and as linguistic tensions. In Olson's poetry, words act as vectors of the kinetics of the page.

"Space" and "language" are related terms in Olson's dictionary: his search for a new language went together with his search for localism in America, while at the same time his sense of place led to a renewal of his language. Olson admired Gertrude Stein because she had two sub-jects: geography and the dictionary (see *Muthologos,* 2:3). These two spheres came together in Olson's poetry, as is indicated by the phrase "localism of language" that Jeremy Prynne coined—to Olson's great liking—in his review of *The Maximus Poems* (see *Muthologos,* 2:105).

The turmoil of the page corresponds to the whole inside the poet's consciousness, giving measure to his awareness that turns place into space. The page as a field of force becomes primary reality just as in electromagnetic field investigations. Connections, not objects, are de-termining. Or, objects cannot be defined without connections. Werner Heisenberg's statement about physics can also be applied to poetic syntax: "[I]n the most recent development of modern physics this [Aristotelian and Cartesian] distinction between matter and form is completely lost, since every field of force contains energy and in so far constitutes matter" (Heisenberg 1958, 130).

Internalization/Intellectualization

The rich texture of Olson's poems demands a participatory (creative) reading from the reader rather than "literate" passive listening. Also, it demands from this reader a certain openness and a willingness to resist and ignore prior expectations, preconceptions, prejudices, and routines of apprehension. The multivalent text, the text characterized by free syntactic and semantic valencies, seems a more faithful transcript of the creative moment, and at the same time promises a more active, activating reading experience.

It is part of Olson's projective stance that no single system is privileged. Poets in the Pound-Williams line, seriously schooled in imagism but aware of its shortcomings and dead ends, too, also experimented with poetries that were marked by varying degrees of formal tightness from improvisation to the most artificial and complicated meters. But no one in this group treated metrical verse and poetic prose as opposite elements of a dichotomy. Instead, they realized that the various forms represent different points on a continuum, going from improvisation (unpremeditated and spontaneous), through the prose poem (still justifiably faithful to experience) and visual free verse (where the physical apearance of the poem punctuates and structures experience), to metered poetry (a crafted form of extraneous ordering). The projective gesture as the basis of poetry lies at the improvisatory end.

Let us accept, though aware of its simplification, the following formula about the levels of the natural process of intellectualization, or intellectual interiorization: 1) level of experiencing; 2) level of interiorizing experience (becoming aware of the nature and significance of experience; meditating upon, ordering, interpreting experience); 3) storing experience (both original and interiorized) in memory. Thus, we can project a continuum from direct to intellectually restructured experience.

All poetry mediates between an internalizing impulse that darts sense perceptions and thoughts inward and an externalizing impulse that seeks to register and describe them. All poetry embodies an interplay of letting go and holding on, a dialogue between spontaneous and artificializing impulses. The most perfectly well-made poem may retain possibilities of projectivism, just as a projective poem may reveal traces of deliberateness; both are born out of the tension between resignation and resolution, between centrifugal (spinning away from its center) and centripetal (interiorizing) forces. However, interplay and tension and dialogue do not imply a balance. And although all poetic forms are "translations" of experience, they perform these translations at different levels, expressing different experiences, at different points on the scale of direct experience/internalizing—intellectualizing/externalizing.

It is impossible not to notice that sense of a return to the performance of direct experience that pervades modern and postmodern poetry. Indeed, this poetry with its dominant naturalizing impulse claims and thematizes a direct connection, a proximity to lived experience; this is the ethos of free verse. I must also stress here the urge of the modern and postmodern poet to uncover the unknown. Poetry of open forms sets out to explore hidden domains/terrains of consciousness. The projective poet insists on writing what he does *not* know. Projective poetry is thus an epistemological activity; it expresses self-interrogation and self-discovery, entering domains of awareness as yet unexplored.

However, the conviction that all these terrains can ultimately be known is missing from Olson's poetics. Accepting Keats's "Negative Capability," and Heisenberg's "uncertainty principle," the poet has doubts concerning the degree to which one can know the world in its totality as well as doubts concerning the degree of explicability of this knowledge in poetry and art. The poem's difficulties may have to be left lying: the poet, critic, and reader achieve "the capability of being in uncertainties, mysteries, doubts, without any irritable reaching after fact and reason."[15] The poet is not *the* sayer; the poem itself is an experience to which the hearer is exposed.

Painters and writers have often described the feeling of facing the void and the unknown, what it feels like to have to start out with no plan in mind, only the blank canvas or page. For D. H. Lawrence, whose paintings hung in Olson's house, the moment of beginning was the most exciting moment: he yearned to disappear by plunging into the canvas:

when you have a blank canvas and a big brush full of wet colour, and you plunge. It is just like diving into a pond—then you start frantically to swim. So far as I am concerned, it is like swimming in a baffling current and being rather frightened and very thrilled, gasping and striking out for all you are worth. The knowing eye watches sharp as a needle; but the picture comes clean out of instinct, intuition and sheer physical action. Once the instinct and intuition gets into the brush-tip, the picture *happens*, if it is to be a picture at all. . . . The struggling comes later. But the picture itself comes in the first rush, or not at all. It is only when the picture has come into being that one can struggle and make it *grow* into completion. (Lawrence, 301)

Closed and metered poetry, on the other hand, does not just *happen:* it is born out of moments of "struggling" from the start. Because it is based on existing formal patterns, such poetry demands by its nature some "fitting" of the thinking process to the particular pattern. As soon as this fitting is attempted, *process* is superseded by *structure* (with some resulting entropy). The poet who works to pattern must follow the example of the known; the subject matter of his poetry can therefore only be what the poet already knows. Such a poet can achieve coherence and wholeness in his well-made poem, and create something that offers itself to thorough and full explication, but this achievement comes at the cost of discovery, insight, vision.

Perhaps it is not a blasphemy to say that poetry acts like a printer connected to a computer, translating and transmitting the various phases of intellectualization, depending on where it is "connected" in the continuum between direct experience and intellectually restructured experience, from spontaneous improvisation at one extreme through formulated statement in metered verse at the other. The intervening stages are projective/dismembered verse, prose poem, and visual poetry.

Improvisation is unpremeditated, unforeseen discourse; it is loyal to experience in the sense that is spontaneous and simultaneous with the composing act. The lack of visual spacing, of prosodic spatiality, seems to be consonant with a lack of a governing focus existing prior to the act of composition.

Visually dismembered and *projective verse* try to remain as loyal to the moment of recognition as possible; they both articulate the thinking/mental process by scoring the arrival of mental blocks into the poet's consciousness on the page, too.

The *prose poem* suggests a continuous flow of composition; it propagates completeness of form and continuity of creative process.

In *visually patterned poetry,* free verse of dismemberment, and various other forms of visual prosody, visuality serves as a way of punctuating experience; this form of attention already seems to structure the poem in a retrospective way.

In *metered poetry,* both metrical and visual form structure the text;

meter is an extraneous ordering device, assigning values, and giving a crafted character and the look of a labored artifice. Experience is translated into intellectual terms; the forces of the world and self are concretized and given form. This kind of poetry is born of a different form of consciousness, being restructured through some interpretive focus, but not without some loss of the original spontaneous energy.

The fundamental difference between poetries at the two ends of the scale is not to be found in prosodic tightness or looseness, but in their closeness to or distance from experience. Meter, as I. A. Richards declares, "acts as the agent of aesthetic distance," and it is for this reason that forms at the improvisational end reflect, in Richards's words, "a change in the regime of consciousness."[16] Modern art and literature share the impulse of shutting the "theoretic eyes," as D. H. Lawrence writes, in order to act as an extension of experiencing, in utmost sincerity. "Art is a form of supremely delicate awareness and atonement—meaning at-one-ness, the state of being at one with the object" (304).

The modern poet pushes back the interiorization phase toward direct experience, and consequently the registration process to an earlier phase, too. Adherent to an ethics of awareness and attention, projective poetry implies a full commitment to sincerity in paying attention to the possibilities of thinking. Sincerity as a bardic virtue is inherent in the attitude of the writer who projects the fluctuations of his mind without imposing his order upon them. Thus composition by field becomes an ethical commitment.

Olson's poetics differs from more traditional theories of labored artistry in that it stresses faculties of attention, listening, and awareness instead of system making, repetition, coherence, wholeness. One-time-only events tend to be as important in spontaneous/projective forms as repetitive events in tight forms. The reader experiences a new pleasure that arises from unpredictability when language is thickened by sound effects and visual effects that will not be echoed later on. This nonrepetitive exploitation of language, together with emphasis and intensity, are the usual virtues of this choice of the poem's form. The projective poet insists on transmitting experience without restructuring it, without one sharp focus and perspective, thus teaching an ethics of awareness and attention instead of catechizing processed ideas.

Chapter Four
Shorter Poems

Earlier Poetic Writings

Those seven pieces that precede the poems of *Y & X* in *Archaeologist of Morning,* the only selection of short poems that Olson authorized for publication during his lifetime, show him as a major poet in emergence. As a series, they serve as an organic prelude to all that Olson will want to say about posture, stance toward reality, methodology for living, apperception of history, and the fullness of living in his later, better-known pieces.

Sherman Paul speaks of a modest beginning, of "stiff and formal" exercises carried out in "tutelage to Williams and Pound," and of a "lack of charged emotions" when discussing these seven poems.[1] True, Olson's indebtedness to Pound and Williams in these poems is obvious; however, we cannot dismiss these poems as only derivative. Pound and Williams did provide the schooling for apprentice Olson, as for so many other beginning poets. For example, the very first poem, "Lower Field—Enniscorthy," contains lines that Olson simply borrowed from Pound, such as the simile of the sheep-soldiers with black leggings, or the final two lines: "Report: over all / the sun." And Olson's large debt to Williams and imagism is also transparent in these preludes. He aims at a direct presentation of the field and thus draws the still life of the sheep-crows-muck-bees-snakes scene ("Lower Field—Enniscorthy") or the lions, salts, grass, muscle, axe, and ox ("A Lion upon the Floor"). These poems are exercises in attention—the attention that is the prerequisite of stance—in the imagist manner.

But we also witness the emergence of a definite stance. Olson's insistence on direct experience is here coupled with his focus on the physicality of being and is directed both inward and outward. He expresses his wish to reestablish man's ties with nature through a return to the senses, to the body, to the elementary constituents of nature: minerals, earth, rock, light. This desire for the "re-naturalization of man," to use Merrill's words (Merrill, 138), permeates all the earlier

poems. In "A Lion upon the Floor," for example, Aztec rituals are
evoked as an example of intense physicality and a way of living consonant with cosmic forces. The alertness of the lion is presented as an
ideal for coincident attention (coincident, that is, of the inner and
outer) and intensive presence as the fraction of moment right before the
lion should spring is depicted. Olson in his teaching voice meets us in
this poem:

> Power and the abstract
> distract a man
> from his own gain
>
> .   .   .   .
> foul his eye
> deprive his hand upon a nape and hip
> of kiss beak claw

"Power and the abstract" are presented as the chief enemies of man who
has lost his ties with nature but who is now perhaps seeking renaturali-
zation; obedience and concreteness are offered as forgotten possibilities.

Love is emerging as a major theme. "Troilus" tries to define "what
love alone is key to, form." (This is a motif Olson will return to in
elaborate detail later in "1, Maximus of Gloucester, to You": "and form
only comes / into existence when / the thing is born.") "Love is not love
with end, with objects lost," the poem proposes. For Olson, love seems
to have nothing to do with finality and results; instead, love is presented as a process, a path, a way, where objects are formed and form is
articulated through attention and presence—"The path, love is the
path."

The next poem, "Only the Red Fox, Only the Crow," continues the
love motif. It is a "will of love" of sorts, handed down to the living by
the dead. The narrator's perspective is presented through the brutally
plastic imagery of bodily deterioration:

> You to whom the spring can return
> when we will merely correlate a worm
> enjoy the envy
> in this blind glance

The lines are powerful, especially because of the unusual angle of what
is demanded and declared. Olson counts on this common human weak-

ness: the appreciation of what is absent, the longing for what is lost. His stress is on the elementary physical joy love may give:

> And when, on summer field
> two horses run for joy
> like figures on a beach
> your mind will find us,

The "envoy" of the poem, "make most of love," given in this context of a dead speaker, is just one way of putting Olson's later imperative concerning resistance to death. "None sang of death" of the Greeks, says "Name-Day Night," another poem elaborating the same theme. The early Greeks did not need reminders of death to achieve fullness of being: they danced, sang of love and war, and were able to partake of cosmic forces with gusto:

> . . . I marked then, and ask now
> what light it is shines in their eyes, what source
> their gusto hath;
> this name-day night these men of Greece disclose
> their eyes shine from outside, take light, shine
> from nature, partake her common force, shine
> by addition, separation,

"The light of the body is the eye, let it be clear" is the way Olson rephrases the same message in the most didactic poem of this sequence, "In the Hills South of Caparneum, Port." In the persona of Jesus, Olson is adding his own propositions to the Old Testament commandments, thus giving a "restatement of the moral dicta of Jesus," as William Aiken puts it.[2] This is a poem that contains such basic Olsoniana as "Take the natural for base / assume your nature as a bird his or the grass." A warning against "any double allegiance" will be emphatically restated later in "The Songs of Maximus" with the powerful lines: "In the land of plenty, have / nothing to do with it." The poem depicts a coming to consciousness in matters of living, the recognition of choice, as well as the choosing itself.

Another early subject is the ocean. "Pacific Lament," is an elegiac poem with Whitmanesque and Eliotic resonances (especially "Out of the Cradle Endlessly Rocking" and *The Waste Land*). In later poems the sea is going to command Olson's historical attention, but already here the embrace of cosmology is present:

> sleep in your black deep
> by water out of which man came
> to find his legs, arms, love, pain.
> Sleep, boy, sleep
> in older arms than hers,
> rocked by an older father;

Y & X

Y & X, Olson's first book of poems, was published in 1948; it contained five poems only, to be rearranged in later collections. The themes here are typically Olsonian, but not yet the formal inventiveness. These poems were written during the three years right after the end of World War II, the period marked by Olson's turn from public office to a poetic career. It was also the period preceding his Black Mountain stay and especially his "Projective Verse" essay. What the poems bear witness to is, however, his intellectual maturity: they record the steps of his becoming aware and conscious of his choice of vocation and of all that this choice entails. Poems such as "The K" and "The Green Man" deal with the process of becoming a poet, of emerging and developing. These pieces appear to have been influenced by Corrado Cagli's friendship and the issues it generated, such as attention ("The Moebius Strip," "Trinacria," "The K") and history ("La Préface").

It is in "The K" where Olson directly gave "his answer": in the coupling of the motifs of emergence and withdrawal ("strategic withdrawal," to use Robert von Hallberg's words[3]). The poem speaks of a "tide in man," whose recognition brings about that obedience to the inner voice, to the calling of the "life within," that he himself was then experiencing. This calling is given cosmic dimensions: the tide is moved by his moon in order to achieve the fuller being expressed by the "tumescent I."

> Take, then, my answer:
> there is a tide in a man
> moves him to his moon and,
> though it drop him back
> he works through ebb to mount
> the run again and swell
> to be tumescent I

"Tumescent I" suggests that the self is in a state similar to the heightened intensity of the body before the sexual act. The word *tumescent* in its tactile quality suggests a coining of two other words: *tumultuous* and *fluorescent*. "Tumescent I" thus suggests the self radiating from fullness and turbulence.

However, "The affairs of men remain a chief concern" for the emerging poet who is withdrawing from the world. First he needs to come to terms with the possibility of an early death made likely by the "fatal male small span" of the father's family. We witness this coming to terms as the acceptance of and obedience to one's "moonward sea": "Assume I shall not," (that is, live to see the year 2000): "Is it of such concern when what shall be is already within the moonward sea?" With his withdrawal from a public career and his turn to the poetic vocation, his attention leaves the world of "romans, hippocrats and christians." He turns, as von Hallberg puts it, from the "government of horses," the anthropocentric cosmologies of "ecco men," and the heliocentrism of the "dull copernican sun" to a geocentric simplicity (von Hallberg 1978, 6):

> Our attention is simpler
> The salts and minerals of the earth return
> The night has a love for throwing its shadows around a man
> a bridge, a horse, the gun, a grave.

The other poem directly related to the problem of emergence is "The Green Man," originally entitled "The Praise of the Fool." A poem of Yeatsian inspiration (borrowing such familiar imagery as fool, stick, and bag), it celebrates his chosen retreat ("Let those who want to, chase a king") and his newly practiced devotion and fidelity in what Yeats would call "passionate syntax."

> And you who go when the green man comes
> who leave your fields,
> go as the dog goes at his heels
> ahead, aside, and always after
> be full of
> loud laughter
>
> Of bitter work and of folly
> cockatrice and cockocolly
> furiously sing!

Cagli's influence emerges again as Olson recalls meeting the Italian refugee painter Corrado Cagli in 1940, in "La Préface." Cagli spoke no

English, but talked "via stones." "La Préface" is a complex poem, responding to World War II as the event expressing the final collapse of our civilization. History is portrayed by reference to the Altamira cave drawings and drawings of Buchenwald—works depicting the same hunting spirit: " 'My name is NO RACE' address / Buchenwald new Altamira cave / With a nail they drew the object of the hunt." In this poem, compared in significance to Yeats's "The Second Coming," Olson makes the statement that new life can be built on this dead civilization of power and ego ("The dead in via / in vita nuova"). Two root persons, Olson and Cagli, of "kindred spirit," choose to begin again, being capable of transforming guns into arms, and thus of building a new locality. They already witness the birth of "the Howling Babe."

> Put war away with time, come into space.
>
> . . . .
>
> It is the radical, the root, he and I, two bodies
> We put our hands to these dead.
>
> . . . .
>
> We are born not of the buried but these unburied dead
> crossed stick, wire-led, Blake Underground
>
> . . . .
>
> The Babe
> the Howling Babe

"The Moebius Strip" and "Trinacria" are also related to Cagli, but their focus falls on the state of attention depicted and practiced by the visual artist. "Trinacria" is a poem that proposes to the warring man naked contact and the force of attention instead of fighting "behind a shield," so that the battle should cease to be an "outside thing." "The Moebius Strip" was directly inspired by Cagli's drawings, and was published on the occasion of an exhibition by the artist, under the title "To Corrado Cagli." Olson presents scenes from the drawings of Cagli, all moments of intensive suspension.

> A man within himself upon an empty ground.
> His head lay heavy on a huge right hand
> itself a leopard on
> his left and angled shoulder.
> His back a stave, his side a hole into the bosom of a sphere.
>
> . . . .
>
> And three or four who danced,

> Their bare and lovely bodies sweep, in round
> of viscera, of legs
> of turned-out hip and glance, bound
> each to other, nested eggs
> of elements in trance.

What the man sitting in the position of leopard alertness and the dancers in trance share is their state of charged attention, when the experience outside and the experience inside are identical and coincident.

In Cold Hell, in Thicket

Olson's second book of poetry, *In Cold Hell, in Thicket*, was published as issue 8 of *Origin* in 1953, while he was rector at Black Mountain College. The volume is structured with precision and care: it is divided into three sections, each defined by some carry-on theme introduced in the prefaratory poem of each section.

Section 1 opens with "La Préface," which, in its new context, seems to be offering new themes in addition to those related to Cagli. The poem assigns universal significance to the personal conflicts that the artists faced after the Second World War. It opens into the tension and counteraction between forces of decay halting the human enterprise on the one hand, and those that nourish and feed man's will to endure on the other.

"The Kingfishers"   "La Préface" is followed by "The Kingfishers," a poem that has won unanimous critical praise. Creeley quotes the poem as a demonstration of the "sole and major content in contemporary American poetry" that Olson's work represents; he insists that the poem has the same presence and force that Mayan glyphs contain ("A Quick Graph," 154). Sherman Paul calls it a position poem, a declarative poem, a cry of emergence (Paul, 1). In Merrill's view, this piece is "the most dense rendering of the Olson posture"; it is "Olson distilled," "a reliable index to the dogmatic complexity of its author" (Merrill, 64).

"If you don't know Kingfishers," Merrill quotes Olson as saying, "You don't have a starter" (*LO,* 63). Indeed, a starter it is: a piece initiating a chain of intellectual reactions, a compendium of his preoccupations at the time of his full emergence as a poet, a starter shooting out axioms, paradoxes, statements that induce the fermenting process

of thinking and meditation. Guy Davenport praises Olson's "philosophical radar" in depicting "a paradigm of the process of continuity
and change"; he claims "The Kingfishers" is "the most modern of
American poems, the most energetically influential text in the last
thirty-five years," a courageous endeavor to resuscitate "a poetic form
worked to death between the late eighteenth and mid-nineteenth centuries," the poetic meditation upon ruins.[4]

What is this energy and American modernity in "The Kingfishers"?
Just looking at it, we can sense something of its power: the text seems
to be fragmented, filling out space in a visual way, with word clusters
in action creating a field. Pound's ideogramic method and Williams's
field-of-action poetics come to mind immediately, but so too does
Eliot's collage architecture as perfected in *The Waste Land* (the poem
also includes echoes from "Prufrock" and the *Four Quartets*). But not
only is the poem's form open and wide: the poem's statements remain
with us as eternal truths uttered by a modern sage. Olson is using his
preaching voice here, but does it in such a way that he is able to
provoke our curiosity in a very basic manner: trusting him, we follow
him throughout the whole process of meditation.

The projectivist technique creates this impact, even though in 1949,
when the poem was written, the term had not yet been coined. Olson
manages to be declarative and convincing at the same time: the reader is
sucked in by the poem because its moments of finality and conclusion
(the declarations) come as provocative resting points in the projective
process. The reader follows exactly those leaps of thought that Olson
went through at the moment of writing. If we do not approach the poem
with the methods we use when solving a puzzle or riddle, but instead
allow ourselves to be carried forward by the collage clusters, our reading
will be valid and revealing. The poem—like many other Olson poems—
closes up in the face of interpretation based on the mechanics of reason
and logos, but opens up for the participant reader, for whom mere
participation in the progressing of the lines is of value and meaning.

"Each of these lines is," Olson wrote of the poem, "a progressing of
both the meaning and the breathing forward, and then a backing up,
without a progress or any kind of movement outside the unit of time
local to the idea" (*Selected Writings,* 23). The progress of syntax and
breathing reveals the meanings. The ideogramic method of creating a
field of poetic objects makes of the poem a verbal activity: it is through
action and process that the writer and reader explore the field of
thought.

"The Kingfishers" neither follows a preconceived pattern, nor elaborates a preconceived idea. Merrill, using the term Olson borrowed from
Franz Kline, calls the poem a "marvelous maneuver," the product of a
writer who "did what he knew before he knew what he did" (Merrill,
86). In order to accomplish this "marvelous maneuver," the writing had
to be simultaneous with the thinking; in other words, creation itself
guided the epistemological inquiry, which the writer had to follow
with "intuitive obedience" (Merrill, 85). "I don't know what I am up
to," Olson admitted in his interview with Merrill while discussing his
rationale for composition by field, "And must stay in that state in order
to accomplish what I have to do."[5] This willingness always to leap
forward into the spheres of the unknown gives a distinct character to
Olson's poetry; it accounts for what many critics and readers consider
its obscurity and difficulty. His poetry is indeed sometimes obscure and
difficult, but at the same time we have to acknowledge that its difficulty often may be traced to our own inability to get rid of old interpretive and critical reflexes. Approached openly, with the willingness to
allow ourseves to be carried in unpredictable directions, Olson's poetry
proves to be the most exciting and courageous adventure.

Burton Hatlen, in his essay soon to be published under the title
"Kinesis and Meaning: 'The Kingfishers' and the Critics,"[6] offers a
critique of contemporary intentional criticism that fails to deal with
such key texts of modern poetry as "The Kingfishers." He refers the
curious reader to eight interpretations of the poem, and suggests that
the many discrepancies between these approaches do not indicate an
ambiguous text with multiple meanings, but rather a fundamental
"unfittingness" of critical discourse to postmodern poetry. By discourse, Hatlen denotes "both a way of talking/writing and a way of
thinking, both a method of exposition and a method of analysis." "The
discourse of modern criticism assumes," he goes on, "that a coherent,
unified perspective on the world must be implicit in any good poem,
and that the task of criticism is to articulate this perspective, draw it
out, 'translate' it into discursive terms." The radically different conclu-
sions of the various critics can be explained by their attempt to uncover
such a "unifying purpose" controlling the sequence of images in the
poem.

The identity of Fernand in the poem is a point, for example, where
critical interpretations diverge; another such point is Mao's figure. And
the evaluation of such details naturally adds up to an evaluative reading
of the poem as a whole. Hatlen shows how some critics (like Paul,

Hallberg, and Kyle) give a "radical reading" in that they see the poem as a "celebration of revolutionary revival," while others (Davenport, Merrill, Combs, Christensen) seem to offer a more "conservative reading" because they find in "The Kingfishers" the "affirmation of conservative values."[7] "These readings," Hatlen points out, "seem to reveal more about the ideological predisposition of the critics themselves than they do about anything that might or might not be going on in Olson's poems."

Hatlen suggests that we rethink the terms in which we talk about poetry, and that we develop a different critical discourse, one that does not try to uncover the "meaning" that the poet "intended" to communicate. In his discussion he unfolds the process of the poem not through an interpretation of image and symbol sequences, but through presenting the poem as "a verbal icon, a kinetic event." Indeed, Hatlen manages to discuss "The Kingfishers" in a way that allows us "simply to accept the poem as it is, without projecting onto it any unnecessary interpretive schema," without assigning any value to the images and their movement. Hatlen urges the reader and the critic to "resist the pull of meaning," and to focus "not on what 'The Kingfishers' 'means' but on what it *does,* how it works as a linguistic event."

"What does not change / is the will to change," the poem begins. This is undoubtedly the most discussed line of the whole poem, although the least original in the sense that it is a rephrasing of Heraclitus, "change is at rest," or in other paraphrases: "change alone is unchanging" or "the will to change is itself changeless."[8] But this "legendary opening line," as Fielding Dawson puts it, reaches an "oblique perfection" through the monosyllabic spacing of breath (126). It sets the tone of the poem, offers the axiom on change and continuity as the paradox of life, a dogma of living. "The opening line," Sherman Paul explains, "is . . . a text for meditation, containing the poem that activity of thought unfolds" and thus "is a summons to action" (Paul, 11). The line is like a mantra, inspiring for contemplation and concentration. The subject of this meditation process shall be human history, its continuity and reality, the possibility for a renewal through knowledge.

Hatlen suggests that the reader inspect both what this first line says and what it does. As a statement, Hatlen claims, it is a "form of categorical proposition," demanding for itself "absolute, universal truth"; it is a "thesis sentence, a generalization which the poem to follow will substantiate." As to what the first line does, Hatlen calls our attention to the physicality of the line as emphasized by the slash mark, by its being a breath-unit broken into two. He also points to the virtuosity that helps Olson divide the line exactly into two parts: the division is perfect whether we count syllables or words (in which case the auxiliary acts as an equals sign, a "passive hinge"). By such simple physicality, the line seems to enact that "opposition-in-unity" which it denotes. The first part of the line, Hatlen explains, "declares an aspiration towards the eternal, the realm of Being, WHAT DOES NOT CHANGE." However, no matter how confident this affirmation is, the second part "declares itself as in all possible ways standing over against the first part: the grammatical mode is positive, the theme is Becoming rather the Being, as we pass from eternity into time, guided by THE WILL TO CHANGE." In using paradox, the most alogical of all rhetorical figures, as the upbeat and thesis of his poem, Olson is, in Hatlen's words, "setting out to enact an alternative to logos, to discourse." By balancing the two parts of the paradox, eternity against time, change against the unchanging, being against becoming, Olson manages to enact the continuous, the process, that which is the "philosophical middle term between the changeless and the changing," to kinetically enact "the opposition-in-unity and the unity-amid-opposition of Being and Becoming."

The poem's architecture uses the dimensions of space and time in a special way, so that it tends toward continuity rather than structure. Its three main parts might suggest some idea of symmetry, provoking expectations of premeditated composition and completeness; such balanced structure, however, is nowhere in the poem. Parts 2 and 3 are decreasing in length, and are much less detailed than part 1 with its four subsections. It is undoubtedly this first part that is most labored upon, containing as it does all the motifs, themes, topics, ideas, and preoccupations that will be treated and varied later on. The four sections of part 1 contain the seeds of everything happening in the poem. Neat structure, finished form with closure, where all the threads are tied—this ideal is completely absent. Instead, ideas are introduced in the first four sections in full detail, with minuteness and multiplicity and are granted open space for interaction. Of course, by the nature of the medium of language, such plurality of propositions necessarily proceeds in a linear order; however, by not tying down the individual threads of assembled materials in the later sections of the poem, Olson manages to keep free the valences of language clusters or chunks of ideas. These units of thought with free valences are offered mental and visual space for unlimited (and often unpredictable) interaction.

Part of this technique is, I think, the immediacy and directness with which Olson turns to new materials. The text is fragmented, with many leaps of thought. But whenever we turn to new materials, we do it with utmost intensity and specificity. With each cut and leap, the poet turns a new rock over, and under each new rock he finds complete life. Olson does not concentrate upon the context; he does not offer transitional passages to facilitate easier understanding. Nor can he have such intentions in view, when his poem was born out of a most faithful following of his own leaping mind. When, after the opening statement, the poem evokes the world of a man after waking, we feel very much submerged into this person's life without knowing much about him:

> He woke, fully clothed, in his bed. He
> remembered only one thing, the birds, how
> when he came in, he had gone around the rooms
> and got them back in their cage, the green one first,
> she with the bad leg, and then the blue,
> the one they had hoped was a male,

There are ten instances of pronouns (*he, they, she*) or pronominal forms (*his, them, their*) in this passage of six lines. The definite article occurs six times in these two sentences. And yet Olson supplies no specified reference, no context. We begin the poem as if we were reading a single page from the middle of a book, or as if we were entering a room in a house, of which the rest was missing. We are presented with the microcosm without the environment of the macrocosm. This is why Hatlen can describe these lines as mysterious and dreamlike, evoking a displaced world defined by the tension of such opposites as past vs. present, sleep vs. rising and acting, remembering vs. doing. The symbolic charge of the birds from the cage is hinted at, but not unfolded; the mystery, without the context of the macrocosm, remains unresolved.

The same holds true of the next unit, the Fernand passage that concludes the first section. The language tends toward the conversational and spontaneous, evoking the verbal kinetics of fragments of conversations overheard at a party. This world is as displaced as the one presented in the previous passage. Hatlen explains the two ways in which dislocation is carried out in this passage: by "making strange" a discursive prosy narrative in the absence of a context and by the use of what Hatlen calls "dislocated language." The incomplete clauses, gram-

matical anomalies, and scattered poetic effects, Hatlen claims, point to
the use of language as plastic medium.

> He had left the party without a word. How he got up, got into his coat,
> I do not know. When I saw him, he was at the door, but it did not matter,
> he was already sliding along the wall of the night, losing himself
> in some crack of the ruins. That it should have been he who said, "The King-
> fishers!
> who cares
> for their feathers
> now?"

> His last words had been, "The pool is slime."

We get a sense of the process of thinning and ending, of some power or
force going out: the man, leaving a party and losing the attention of the
others, seems constantly pulled into the mystery of the ruins and the
problematics of how a civilization can end by its own nature, in an
organic way ("The pool is slime").

In the next section the field of the ideogram becomes spacious and
wide, opening the possiblity for interaction of a wide range of elements. We witness the evocation of "the E on the stone," fragments
from Mao Tse-tung's speech given to the Chinese Communist party,
quotations from the *Encyclopaedia Britannica*'s entry on the kingfisher,
and Olson's own mental runs on the features and nesting practices of
the kingfisher. He contemplates the bird's natural history and the
lessons it offers concerning human history and the fate of civilizations.
Concepts like polis and community, constancy and change, east and
west, scientific precision and mythical legends, the building of civilizations as layers of history—they all interact on the page and within
the mind of the reader, and bring into motion a whole field of
thought clusters in the manner of Pound's magnetic rose in the steel
dust. This section's turmoil activates the field, but refuses to attach
interpretation and value to the complexity of the ideogram. Hatlen
refers to the darkness, decay, and corruption implied by recalling the
legends around the kingfisher as examples of "inescapable symbolic
overtones" that cannot be read as "signalling any single attitude."
"The Kingfishers," Hatlen emphasizes, "cannot be reduced to a single
interpretive schema, whether 'conservative' or 'radical' "; "the poem
enacts a kinetic movement which transcends and absorbs into itself
such ideological opposites."

Section 3 of part 1 picks up the theme of the perishability and exhaustion of civilizations, and the poet allows himself to be carried into complex speculation. Behind the goings and comings of civilizations Olson sees two possibilities, natural death or murder. Natural death occurs, when peoples' attention turns toward something other than the nourishing of civilization, and murder is the result of conquest.

> When the attentions change / the jungle
> leaps in
>   even the stones are split
>   they rive
> Or,
> enter
> that other conqueror we more naturally recognize
> he so resembles ourselves

The conqueror has no understanding of the world to be conquered: it is like a wild fantasy world to him, with strange, unknown creatures, and with savage-looking priests panicking at the arrival of newcomers. And rightly so, because the conqueror is Cortés, and the civilization doomed to die is that of the Totomac Indians. The perspective of the historical account now opens into the universal and generic present:

> And all now is war
> where so lately there was peace,
> and the sweet brotherhood, the use
> of tilled fields.

Section 4 is loaded with meanings. All that Olson has suggested about change and continuity, death and rebirth, attention and conquest, falls into place here. The concept that gives new meaning to all the others is "feed-back"; that is, the rose governing the steel dust.

"Not one death but many," the section starts out. The source is Heraclitus, but also, as Sherman Paul has showed, Pablo Neruda's *The Heights of Macchu Picchu* ("y no una muerte, sino muchas muertes") (Paul, 20). The perspective is here specified: the problematics of change is not treated within nature ("not accumulation but change"), but in history through the individual and the personal, where "the feed-back is / the law." Heraclitus's famous dogma ("Into the same river no man steps twice") is explained by Norbert Wiener's feedback concept and Whitehead's philosophy of process. Feedback as a method of correction in both history and personal action explains change as the only possible form of permanence, when attention becomes the force that puts change in continuity—"To be in different states without a change / is not a possibility." Communication and control are listed as forms of feedback, both involving the message about the processural nature of reality. "In a universe of process," as Merrill explains the proposition of feedback and change, "of incessant change, man must assume a posture that will tap rather than obstruct the inherent energy of that change" (Merrill, 78). Creativity stems from the obedience of man to forces in change, which obedience takes the form of communication through attention or feedback. Control, although also a force in history (especially during conquests and conquerings), is unable to conceive of reality as change and process. The "too strong grasping of it," which Keats described as the opposite of "Negative Capability," forecloses the process and "loses it," that reality which

> is change, presents
> no more than itself
>
> And the too strong grasping of it,
> when it is pressed together and condensed,
> loses it
>
> This very thing you are

Part 2 of "The Kingfishers" turns to Mexico for lessons about renewal and about the repossession of that which power, control, and "the grasping of it" lost. The location this part evokes is an Aztec burial ground, where the dead are buried in a sitting posture, ready to "rise, act." This site is home not only to the Aztec dead, but also to the conquistador spirit, to "pudor pejorocracy" and dirtiness. On the stalks of Aztec culture "pejorocracy" climbed. The Aztec seem still to be more alive in their sitting posture than their conquerors, whose spirit "crawls / below."

Sherman Paul praises the poet for "escaping the Western Box in which he felt Pound was trapped" (Paul, 28). Indeed, Olson seems to have found his "kins" outside the Greco-Roman tradition.

> I am no Greek, hath not th'advantage.
> And of course, no Roman:

> he can take no risk that matters,
> the risk of beauty least of all.
> But I have my kin, if for no other reason than
> (as he said, next of kin) I commit myself,

He commits himself, like Rimbaud, to the earth and the rocks, and all that "was slain in the sun." In other words, the speaker interested himself in history, archaeology, physicality, and ritual. The question "shall you uncover honey / where maggots are" might have Samson's riddle as its source. It certainly condenses the central image of the poem into the metaphor of life feeding on death, the paradox of continuity and change.

> I pose you your question:
> shall you uncover honey / where maggots are?
> I hunt among stones

The concluding sentence falls into three parts grammatically: it refers to the actor of the activity, to the action itself, and to the locality where the action takes place. By using the transitive verb *hunt* as if it was intransitive (without an object), the hunting process is thematized as one where the significance of the activity of search itself towers over the urge and hunger for the object hunted. Search in its continuity and kinesis is given priority over the finality of the resulting act of finding—a principle that the poem as a whole seems to be reenacting in a radical way.

The other poems of *In Cold Hell, in Thicket* expose other facets of the process of this hunt, search, struggle leading to the creative act. We are participants in a clarification process that Olson is going through: clarifying his relation to history, the poetic tradition, and the knowledge of the relationship of man to his environment.

History   "At Yorktown" and "There Was a Youth Whose Name Was Thomas Granger" are the two directly historical poems. "At Yorktown" speaks of the vital presence of history and death in a plain manner: "At Yorktown the church / at Yorktown the dead / . . . are live." The poem uses bold images of physical disintegration ("the dead / are soil," "heels / sink in") as a way of depicting the sphere or dimension behind everyday scenes that are not often associated with death: "the hollows / are eyes are flowers, the heather."

In "There Was a Youth Whose Name Was Thomas Granger" Olson critiques the world he inherited by evoking an incident in American history, the execution of Thomas Granger, aged 16 or 17, in 1642. The charge against him was "drunkennes & uncliannes / incontinencie betweene persons unmaried" and "that which is worse," bestiality. The verdict of the judges of Plymouth Plantation was death, naturally. Olson, declaring his disagreement with this death sentence, addresses "Mr. Bradford" in an argument that incorporated period documents. Written around early 1947, the poem bears traces of Olson's involvement in Pound's trial, I think. In "This Is Yeats Speaking," he attacked the same "department called Justice" and made clear his views on the absurdity of putting a person on trial, of a court doing justice. The poem is an instance of Olson's own "feedback" on history, his method of correcting the hypocrisy of "pejorocracy."

"La Chute," although somewhat stylized and full of language mannerisms, proposes a different angle on history: that of the survivor of some catastrophe or tragedy ending this cycle of history. The survivor is a poet, who seems to have gained his strength to resist death from poetry, that is, from his lute and drum.

We find a different kind of historical fate in "The Leader"; here the person of strength, originality, and inner power has to face death as a consequence of his deeds. The leader, in whom critics see Orpheus, Dionysus, and Christ, is slain and devoured by his contemporaries who show no understanding of his historical role; his generosity, love, and tranquillity only provoke deeds of hate—his murder.

Olson's relationship to history and the past is always that of involvement. This is how he described this relationship in 1950:

There are only two live pasts—your own (and that hugely includes your parents), and one other which we don't yet have the vocabulary for, because the West has stayed so ignorant, and the East has lived off the old fat too long. I can invoke it by saying, the mythological, but it's too soft. . . . I have spent most of my life seeking out and putting down the "Laws" of these two pasts, to the degree that I am permitted to see them (instead of the boring historical and evolutionary one which the West has been so busy about since Thucydides) simply because I have found them in the present, my own and yours, and believe that they are the sign of a delightful new civilization of man ahead. (*Additional Prose*, 39–40)

"The Moon Is the Number 18" fuses these two layers of history, the personal and that "other," on the occasion of his mother's death. A poem of grief and bitterness, it blends traditional death and life images with tarot symbolism, as altered by his own imagination. The occasion of the poem is deeply personal, intimate even, but the poet opens his grief to cosmic dimensions guided by his inner need to interpret personal history in terms of the occult.

The moon, a traditional image of death, is seen as the planet that, although itself dead, is hosting the dead. It is a grinning and unmoveable god, served by otherworldly blue dogs and the crablike rays of the night.

> is a monstrance,
> the blue dogs bay,
> and the son sits,
> grieving
>
> . . . .
>
> The blue dogs rue,
> as he does, as he would howl, confronting
> the wind which rocks what was her, while prayers
> striate the snow, words blow
> as questions cross fast, fast
> as flames, as flames form, melt
> along any darkness
>
> Birth is an instance as is a host, namely, death

Here Olson blends personal, occult, and Catholic images without symbolic or metaphorical intention. The different image layers do not interpret each other, but instead share the space of this complex death/moon ideogram. Olson's unhesitating trust in the possibility of this fusion is linguistic: the *moon* looks like a *mon*strance on Cagli's drawing of the eighteenth Tarot card (which accompanied the poem on its first publication), while it can *host* the dead as the monstrance hosts the *host* of the eucharist.

Opposed to this death-land is the red tower, of waters and fire, life confronting the wind with prayer, words and fire. This tower of watching, moving, and substance is capable of resisting death and the "dirty moon" of "sortilege" because it can stand up against it with words, articulation, and conjecture.

In the red tower
in that tower where she also sat
in that particular tower where watching & moving are,
there,
there where what triumph there is, is: there
is all substance, all creature
all there is against the dirty moon, against
number, image, sortilege—

alone with cat & crab,
and sound is, is, his
conjecture

Another poem that aims at a blending of personal history and that
"other" history is "An Ode on Nativity," which Olson wrote in celebration of his daughter's birth. As such, it fits into the tradition of nativity
poems and poems written upon the births of daughters and sons to
poets, such as Yeats's "A Prayer for My Daughter." However, the
celebration is not occasioned simply by the daughter's birth; her birth
generates certain ideas and emotions about Olson's own city of birth,
Worcester, and initiates a winding speculation on the daughter's "second birth."

"I, by the way, am celebrating the city of my birth, which I have
only done, I believe, in this poem—which is Worcester, Massachusetts," Olson announced before reading the poem in Berkeley in 1965
(*Muthologos* 1:102–2). His celebration proceeds in a typically Olsonian
way: by going through details and particulars such as the skating pond,
the Sawyer lumber company, the buried Blackstone River, the hills
upon which Winthrop wished to set up his city. Worcester speaks to
Olson, it "jangles" and "rings / in & out of / tune." But Worcester as
the location of personal history seems more relevant to the poem for the
family driving on the highway. Two significant childhood incidents
concerning some kind of fire in the "sky's lights" are recalled.

    . . . this boy, once,
    the first time he saw her whole halloween face northeast
    across the skating pond as he came down to the ice, December
    his seventh year.
    . . . .

        (The same year, a ball of fire
        the same place—exactly through

    the same trees
    was fire:
            the Sawyer lumber company yard
            was a moon of pain, at the end of itself,
            and the death of horses I saw burning,
            fallen through the floors
            into the buried Blackstone River the city
            had hidden under itself, had grown over

"An ode" is a projective poem depicting the state of awareness when "all cries rise" in the poet, when "all things rise," and he is recording this emergence of memories, wishes, attitudes. He allows images of his father's funeral to surface, and incidents his grandmother told him about similar steel mill fires where the grandfather "rolled wild in the green grass." An archaeological excavation of the personal is going on here, a dig into the poet's deepest self:". . . tale of any one of us stormed or quieted / by our own things, what belong, tenaciously, / to our own selves." These are tales that cradle, or *crèche*, as the poem phrases it, our second birth, the birth that really matters according to Olson. Before the second birth, one carries one's body as the close, in the "medieval sense: the quarter, or the holy quarter" (*Muthologos*, 1:105), the cradle, of the second birth that shall give form to that which one is the content of.

        . . . the close
        which can be nothing more and no thing else
        than that which unborn form you are the content of, which you
        alone can make to shine, throw that like light
        even where the mud was and now there is a surface
        ducks, at least, can walk on.

This is the point, second birth, when the on and off light/season/time turns into a continuous, intensive shine and vision.

"What shall be my daughter's second birth?" This is a tormenting question, especially because of the "male small span." Olson, being a good father, knows that fathers are needed until this second birth only, whether by daughters or poets. "I am a perfect father until I'm not," he said of this father-problem at the Berkeley reading (*Muthologos*, 104). He is a perfect father until he needs to be one, until the choice is made between ignoring or experiencing the light. That is how real nativity happens, the poem concludes.

> . . . is there any birth
> any other splendor than
> the brilliance of the going on, the loneliness
> whence all our cries arise?

Tradition   This motif of fathering and second birth leads us to the next cluster of poems, those preoccupied with tradition.

The three poems in the "ABC" series give articulation to Olson's artistic independence. Although the title of the series has Poundian echoes, only the first one, "ABC's," seems to declare Olson's allegiance to the Pound tradition. It is significant that Pound is praised in opposition to Eliot only, as the pun expresses: Eliot is "reverend *re*verse," while "Pound / is verse."

"ABC's (2)" and "ABC's (3—for Rimbaud)" express Olson's break from Pound and Williams too. The charge against Pound is his use of static imagery, lacking in motion and momentum, "coiled or unflown / in the marrow of the bone," his hesitancy to penetrate "in that wood where shapes hide," and his diverting the boat "to avoid the yelping rocks." The attack on Williams is perhaps more brutal: both his images (rain, tent, grass, birds, wire, "the Passaic of orange peels," cats, fruits, beauty) and his attitudes (trillings, cleanings, balloons) are mocked. Olson charges that "the dyes of realism" have misled us.

> Why not the brutal, head on?
> Fruits, beauty? to want it
> so hard? Who
> can beat that life
> into form, who
> is so hopeful—who
> has misled us?

Olson demands brutal truth, powerful words, not just mouths biting empty air. The ideal is the act of "scouring," the verbal expression of the urge for deep examination involving even violence, an obsession for precise reports, "the extension of claritas."

He deals with his role as both father to a younger poet and son of an older in the poem bearing the long title "To Gerhardt, there among Europe's things of which he has written us in his 'Brief an Creeley and Olson.' " Olsons admits his paternity of the young German poet Rainer Maria Gerhardt, his "Bear-son," but refuses to remain Pound's son. He refuses the tradition of both Eliot and Pound and urges the young poet to first find his fathers ("stay on the prowl") and then gain his own independence and strength to leave them:

> Help raise the bones
> of the great man,
>
> .   .   .   .
>
> On the way to your fathers,
> join them

Time, especially past time, however, is not to remain a constant preoccupation: life is to be lived not in time, but in space, in the present of particulars, where the past is present not as history and tradition but as source. Olson gives the young poet the present, "simplicities," "a rod of mountain ash," and ruins as sources for knowledge. All this amounts to one proposition: "For the problem is one of focus, of the field as well as the point of / vision: you will solve your problems best / without displacement." "To Gerhardt" is a significant poem born out of Olson's experience with the Maya. Powerfully, he is passing on the knowledge he gained in Mexico about space and field, the present of particulars and simplicities, the power of perception and focus for restoring man's displacement in the world.

Knowledge   At this time, in the early 1950s, Olson's preoccupation more and more shifted from tradition, artistic dependence, and independence, to the sources, modes, and ways of knowing, and to those cultures, like the Mexican or pre-Socratic Greek, that have built their epistemology on participatory experiences.

"A Discrete Gloss," for example, meditates upon the human universe born out of the fusion of inner and outer experiences, and upon the necessity of attentive obedience in order to recognize such experiences. "Whatever sits outside you" and all that "actually goes on within" are governed by the laws of the same "tide," so that the inner gives emphasis to the outer, and the outer is properly perceived when it has some relevance to the outer.

> In what sense is
> what happens before the eye
> so very different from
> what actually goes on within . . .
>
> .   .   .   .

> Your eye, the wanderer, sees more.
> Or do you know what it focuses on, what happens
> somewhere else, where, say, the sea
> is more sea,

When inner and outer experiences complement each other, man is capable of stepping out of his otherwise rigid patterns of thought, of understanding those "who do not take Saturday and Sunday off," of seeing all that richness in the worlds that otherwise would remain hidden.

> . . . human birds
> with wings which only once
> (in Giotto's hands) made
> black and orange sense?

Proprioception is the phenomenon Olson is engaged in here: the way inner and outer stimuli are received, the difference that perception makes inside, "Interiors, / and their registration" ("ABC's"). The first requirement for effective proprioception is, for Olson, the full and detailed perception of our environment, for which "A Discrete Gloss" gives a lesson. The poem "Knowing All Ways, Including the Transposition of Continents" expresses Olson's insistence on accurate perception and the faithful rendering of this perception in poetry.

> . . . Image
> can be exact to fact, or
> how is this art twin to what is,
> what was,
> what goes on?

"Today / I serve beauty of selection alone," he writes. The fundamental importance of perception lies in its being capable of selecting from man's environment. Perception, and its accurate rendering by the twin method of the image, becomes the major faculty for building and knowing our human universe. It is through the "little brains" of the senses that man turns his original condition, "unselectedness," into "selectiveness," as described in the essay "Human Universe."

Man's various relationships with his environment are treated in the book. An unusually idyllic, nutritive relationship is presented in "A Round & A Canon." The poem describes two adjacent incidents, in

metonymic relationship with each other: the poet swinging his daughter and a bird dying. One is immediately reminded of another swing
poem, Williams's "Portrait of a Lady," but this association is soon
weakened: in Olson's piece there is no reference to sexuality; the excitement comes from the little girl's full pleasure in the dynamics of
motion. She is capable of completely giving herself over to the dialec-
tics of the swing; her unconsious glory is that she fully obeys the tidal
kinetics of the wind having "this affection" for her—"a lovely bird of a
wild human motion." The poet shows a similar admiration for the bird,
having "his own world, his own careful context, those / balances." The
bird is the chii-mi described in "Mayan Letters," where her strength,
vitality, and capacity to survive are presented. Although she dies in this
poem, the poet's admiration for her mobile obedience is not lessened.

Olson proposes a similar kinetic ideal of man as agent in "Concerning Exaggeration, or How, Properly, to Heap Up."[9] Activity, the highest human ideal, is defined here as the process of moving toward form.

> . . . Dignity
> is not to be confused with realism, is not found
> (he was canny enough to say)
> in the straight-on
>
>   however much it does lie
> in particulars—as distorted as an instant is, is
> content. And its form? How shall you find it
> if you are not, in like degree, allowable, are not
> as it is, at least, in preparation for
> an equal act?

Man who is not in touch with the phenomenal world through the
agency of creativity, finds himself in isolation, estranged and out of
place. He is the "wrong man" of "Move Over," who, unable to resist
death, lets "the death-blow in."

Man necessarily finds himself in the isolation of his own rational
world. "Man is no creature of his own discourse," Olson states in "A
Discrete Gloss." A whole poem, "La Torre," is about man's isolation
caused by his own construct, discourse. The poem celebrates the fall
and destruction of this tower of structures, walls, laws, forms—that is,
the tower of rational and discursive order. With its destruction light
that was previously walled out can now shine through, and images of

order can disappear. With the tower gone, old reflexes lose their significance too: the gesture of "grabbing hold of" gives way to "standing
clear," while the rational and discursive towering over man's knowing
gives way to the position of being "beached," or *grounded* in space and
experience.

> Stand clear!
>
> . . . .
>
> Where there are no walls
> there are no laws, forms, sounds, odors
> to grab hold of
>
> Let the tower fall!
> Where space is born
> man has a beach to ground on

With the destruction of the tower, man shall find new strength nour-
ished by a direct contact with his environment: he will be able to wear
his own flesh, will perceive the "laden air" and "fragrant sea," will be
able to live fully in the familiar world of his human universe. It shall be
his real nativity, his second birth into the world of particulars and
physicality.

"The Praises" "The Praises" merits discussion in greater detail than generally possible in this study. This is a powerful and
complex poem on the nature of knowledge after the destructon of the
tower, on the power of understanding, and also on the relationship of
power and knowledge. Speaking of Olson's intellectual elitism, Robert von Hallberg observes that he never really wrote for a large audience and explains this policy as a poetic response to political power
and expansionist policy:

the imminence of an American political empire made Olson leave government,
the prospect of an American intellectual imperium showed him a way to go as
a poet. . . . To write a poetry intended to "fit audience find, though few" may
be a kind of arrogance; but it should be recognized that historical pressures, in
the seventeenth century as well as in the twentieth, may demand a choice
between what is crudely called elitism and silence. In 1950 Olson published
"The Praises," arguing that only elites preserve knowledge, and that knowledge and political power are essentially identical. (von Hallberg 1978, 23)

Olson, as Hallberg shows, used two basic sources: Plutarch's *Moralia* and Matila Ghyka's *The Geometry of Art and Life*. From these books he gained materials concerning the Pythagorean Brotherhood, their secret of the dodecahedron and their betrayal, Plato's numerological theories, the Fibonacci number series, Ammonius's discussion of Apollo's titles of epiphany, and Antiochus's victory over the Galates. The title itself is revealing: taken from Plutarch's essay, it refers to Ammonius's warning against any single explanation of the universe. To those who believe that the number 5, or the fifth letter of the alphabet, is of special mystical significance, Ammonius suggests: "every one of the numbers will provide not a little for them that wish to sing its praises."[10]

The poem gives the various treatments of the secrets and mysteries man is capable of knowing. First Olson speaks about the status of the number 5 in the Pythagorean Brotherhood, for whom the "five solid figures" of the dodecahedron, a mathematical construct, gave the explanation of the universe: "the Sphere of the Universe arose from / the dodecahedron." The number 5 became the guide in military maneuvers too, and with its supernatural power it helped Antiochus, who believed in its divine secret, win his battle against the Galates. Then Olson goes on with the power of 5 in giving rational explanation: he shows how the Fibonacci number series (by which Filius Bonacci tried to approach *phi,* the golden section) is behind the organic architecture of various plants and animal anatomy.

> its capital law in the distribution of
> leaves seeds branches on a stem (ex.,
> the ripe sun-flower)
>
> the ratios $\frac{5}{8}$, $\frac{8}{13}$
> in the seed-cones of fir-trees,
> the ratio $\frac{21}{34}$
> in normal daisies
>
> Pendactylism is general in the animal kingdom.

He lists other instances of pentagonal symmetry: star and jellyfish, the sea urchin, the briar rose, and the passion flower. At this point we are led to believe that it is the golden section, the dodecahedron, or the Fibonacci series that Olson considers the secret. But, as the title warns

us, "praises" are due to numbers and letters other than 5 or E. "Here we
must stop," Olson states; the rational mind must be halted before it
goes too far indulging its desire to explain the universe. Nature looks
explainable only so far "as it is allowed to a mortal to know," for there
are many exceptions to the pentagonal rule: crystals, lilies, tulips, the
hyacinth, minerals in general, the malachite, all these associated with
the feminine mystery:

> o, that's not fair, let
> woman keep her jewels, odd man
> his pleasure of her glow, let
> your lady Nephritite
> pumice her malachite, paint
> her lids green against the light

For although the Pythagoreans, according to Plutarch, expected to
know the nature of man and woman by associating them with 2 and 3,
the sum giving number 5 again (man being the first odd, and woman
the first even number), there remain the mysteries that no number
sequence can explain (see von Hallberg 1978, 223–24, note 32).

The poem is a testament to knowledge and to the unknowable at the
same time. It explains the power the intellectual elite gained through
its knowledge, but it also explains the fall of this intellectual elite
caused by its conviction that its knowledge gave it complete and ultimate explaining power.

Olson uses Ammonius to differentiate the four kinds of knowledge
leading to epiphany: the inquiry, the disclosing, the full knowledge,
and the conversationalist mode of *leskenoi,* which he considers superior
to all other forms, including knowing:

> The last, and triumphant mode, I leave, as he leaves it,
> untranslated: when men are active, enjoy thought, that is to say
> when they talk, they are LESKENOI

For the *leskenoi,* those who are active and who enjoy thought, possess
something that the knowers do not have: they know that real knowledge includes the acceptance of the unknowable, the mysterious, the
irrational, the enigmatic. They know that no one number or letter or
sign can reveal the secret for the limited human mind:

> You would have a sign. Look:
> to fly? a fly can do that;
> to try the moon? a moth
> as well; to walk on water? a straw
> precedes you

The purpose of human knowledge is not to achieve complete understanding, not to unlock secrets and reveal mysteries and irrational
enigmas, but to pursue the process of active inquiry itself, and to
influence actions. This is Olson's ideal of thoughtful action.

> Sd he:
>   to dream takes no effort
>   to think is easy
>   to act is more difficult
> but for a man to act after he has taken thought, this!
> is the most difficult thing of all

"Essentially, this is Olson's understanding of the social role of the
thinker," according to Hallberg; "the point of successful intellectual
career—such as that of Apollonius of Tyana—is to influence men of
political power. . . . action will be hollow and merely materialist un-
less it follows from an ideology" (von Hallberg 1978, 25).

The secret and value needs to be passed on *as* secret and value,
without any loss, not treated as a riddle to be uncovered.

> What has been lost
> is the secret of secrecy, is
> the value, viz., that the work get done, and quickly,
> without the loss of due and profound respect for
> the materials

Once the secret is not contained but is dispersed, destruction follows:
"dirty time" comes, "mu-sick" and "pejorocracy," with "too many having too little / knowledge," and the "mob" takes over.

Olson states his views on the interrelationship of knowledge and
action: not only must action follow from thought and knowledge, but
it is equally important that knowledge be used in action; the relationship is mutual, the necessity is two-sided. It is as necessary to act after
taking time for thought, as it is to pass on knowledge "for use":

> What is necessary is
> containment,
> that that which has been found out by work may, by work be passed on
> (without due loss of force)
> for use
>   USE

"It is a sense of *use,*" Creeley stresses in connection with this passage, "which believes knowledge to be necessarily an *active* form of relation to term, . . . it is knowledge used as a means to relate, not separate."[11] Von Hallberg hears political resonances in these lines, especially because of the term *containment,* and its echoes in the American foreign policy of the late 1940s. Apart from being the justification of Olson's intellectual elitism, the term *containment* seems indeed to refer to his disdain for American expansionist military policy. Olson's belief in the strength of the policy of intellectual containment can, I think, be traced back to Pound's controversial stand against Americans fighting on foreign land.

When a cultural elite gives up its containment, the poem explains, the secret is lost and the mob takes over. Only mere luck accounts for the survival of a few capable of preserving the secret, and passing it on to Plato. This image of partial death makes the first line of the poem meaningful: "She who was burned more than half her body skipped out of death."

"In Cold Hell, in Thicket"   The poem that lends its title to the whole collection also deals with knowing and understanding, expecially with man's possibilities for finding his way in the thickets of this world. "In Cold Hell, in Thicket" is a grand depiction of the human condition of being locked into this thicket, as well as of the desperate struggle of man to build a wagon to carry him out.

The poem carries out its argument about knowing the world and the self in a projective way, in the manner Olson suggested as "living out" in one's personal life. "We live out, until there isn't any, the argument of our own being," he once said (*Muthologos,* 1:102). The argument concerns creativity and the mapping of exterior and interior hell. "[T]he whole area of how we now live, or can live, is part of Mr. Olson's attack," Creeley said of the poem.[12]

The first passage delineates the problem, giving a kind of outline of the themes to be touched on:

> In cold hell, in thicket, how
> abstract (as high mind, as not lust, as love is) how
> strong (as strut or wing, as polytope, as things are
> constellated) how
> strung, how cold
> can man stay (can men) confronted
> thus?

The opening situation presents man confronting a thicket world with the following parameters: it is abstract (nonphysical, nonparticular), strong (a world supported by beams or a frame resisting pressure), strung (with a weblike interior, of wires and threads intertwining), and cold. This environment generates a feeling of confusion and numbness, as well as helplessness—man is easily "tossed up" and knocked down. Olson phrases his dilemma: how can man raise himself by his acts (or, if he is a poet, by his words) above this hell?

> God, that man, as his acts must, as there is always
> a thing he can do, he can raise himself, he raises
> on a reed he raises his
>
> Or, if it is me, what
> he has to say

The speaker seems to be in the environs of a gothic fort arching above the scene, giving a physical proof of man's capacity for "raising" himself by creativity. The observer in the thicket is trying to find a way to grasp this fort intellectually; he wants to know and understand, to "make out" what he sees in space.

> In hell it is not easy
> to know the traceries, the markings
> (the canals, the pits, the mountings by which space
> declared herself, arched

We are confronted by a spot in the thicket of wilderness that managed to raise itself, a fort that articulated space so that space declared itself. This architectural declaration the poem associates with the example of Nut, the Egyptian sky-goddess or goddess of space, arching above her lover-brother, Geb, god of earth. This image, however, only makes the

poet feel his own confusion more vividly; he is tormented by being
unclear and is frustrated at his condition.

> in this brush, stands
> reluctant, imageless, unpleasured, caught in a sort of hell, how
> shall he convert this underbrush, how turn this unbidden place
> how trace and arch again
> the necessary goddess?

The next section suggests some ways of "raising" above the thicket;
it might be put to "use" by "knivings" into paths or carvings or the
building of some wagon or other "vessel fit for / moving." If the
creative gesture of "trace and arch" is not carried out here in space, then
the dimension of time takes over, accumulating "dissolving bones" in
the embrace of mud.

Section 3 turns inward, pursuing knowledge of the self, of identity:
"Who am I but by a fix, and another, / a particle, and the congery of
particles carefully picked / one by another." "Fix," the determination of
one's position, is approached spatially, through an awareness of spatial
particles. Intense fidelity to experience, attention to physical details is,
Olson suggests, the only way for man to raise himself, to "trace and
arch," to leave the abstract and cold hell:

> as in this thicket, each
> smallest branch, plant, fern, root
> —roots lie, on the surface, as nerves are laid open—
> must now (the bitterness of the taste of her) be
> isolated, observed, picked over, measured, raised
> as though a word, an accuracy were a pincer!

This fixing with merciless accuracy is considered to be "the almost
impossible," especially because "hell now / is not exterior." The thicket
lies inside as well as outside one's self,

> is not to be got out of, is
> the coat of your own self, the beasts
> emblazoned on you
>
> . . . .
>   . . . Who
> can endure it where it is, where the beasts are met,
> where yourself is, your beloved is, where she

> who is separate from you, is not separate, is not
> goddess, is, as your core is,
> the making of one hell

There are no clear boundaries between oneself, the beasts, the beloved, the goddess, what is separate and what is not. And, by the same token, no clear boundaries exist between the inside and the outside thicket, and especially between hell and paradise inside. Olson expresses his insistence on knowing and creating, and refuses evaluating.

> That it is simple, what the difference is—
> that a man, men, are now their own wood
> and thus their own hell and paradise
> that they are, in hell or in happiness, merely
> something to be wrought, to be shaped, to be carved, for use, for
> others

The concept of "use" (for others) is always coupled with the concept of obeying for Olson: only an obedient relationship with one's environment, that which acknowledges its laws and demands, can provide nourishment for creativity. Without wavering, the poet's wagon transports him out of hell into precision and claritas: "precise as hell is, precise / as any words, or wagon, / can be made." The poem, unfolding in a projective way, indeed acts as a wagon of words leading us out of the thicket of confusion and frustration.

The Distances

This is the last book of short poems that was published during Olson's lifetime—the last one, apart from *Maximus,* of course, to contain new poems. *The Distances* came out in 1960, when Olson was 49 years old; as such, it is the poetic product of the mature middle years, especially for a late starter like Olson.

The volume collects 21 poems of which only half are new. With the new arrangement, however, Olson creates a new organism that carries new messages and meanings. Olson's choice of poems from the previous collection tells us a lot about how he felt about his work and about his sense of direction. The principles behind the poet's selection seem quite clear: he incorporated those poems which he could use as the foundation when building this new volume. He chose poems that strengthened and reinforced the overall intention of the new volume: the presentation and bridging of human "distances." The volume emerges as the product of an artistic purification process with each of the 21 poems dealing with some aspects of these distances, gaps, and separations. Olson's poetic interests are channeled by an intense focusing of attention to phenomena related to distances. The thrust of the volume is sharply pronounced; the reader senses a powerful distillation of poetic themes and preoccupations.

The "distances" Olson is interested in correspond to the dualisms and dichotomies he describes in the essays; those, for example, between body and soul, logos and tongue, physical and spiritual/mental. These dualisms occur in the poems as separations in various forms: between thought and action, word and image, form and meaning, past (history, tradition) and present, time and space, consciousness and the unconscious, inner and outer, self and world, death and life. The poems urge a complex healing process; Olson wants us to be aware of these unmanageable gaps, to be able to explain historically these civilizational disjunctions, to desire to go back intellectually to those roots and orgins where the gaps do not yet exist, and to recharge the energies through which original unities can be reestablished.

This context sheds new light on the old poems. "The Kingfishers," like a grand overture, opens the volume, announcing that incessant change that brings about slime and corruption, the dirtiness of pejorocracy, the exhaustion of energy, and ultimately the split between man and the world. The "ABC's," the next poems in the sequence, are not simply clarifications of poetic allegiance and independence, but act as a statement (with Poundian associations) about language purification and the rudiments of language use. By joining forces with Pound and Williams against Eliot, Olson suggests a battle against the distortion and "bastardization" of language, as well as a return to speech, direct perception, and language as action. Through the repossession of the primeval lexical energies of words, Olson hopes to discard the form/content and world/image dichotomies. The two historical poems, "There Was a Youth Whose Name Was Thomas Granger" and "At Yorktown," seem to reveal new kinds of distances. The story of Thomas Granger serves as a particular instance in which a pharisaical sense of superiority punishes "sin" and "wickedness" with bold certainty as something alien. The present that generations inherit shall remain irretrievably foreign, Olson suggests, as long as man continues to distance himself from his own past.

"The Praises," with its sense of loss and dispersion, fits well into this thematic sequence. It is one of those rare pieces where the healing of the split or fracture is suggested; this healing is accomplished through active knowledge put to use, through thought enjoyed and passed on, where a pre-Socratic sense of the world adopted by the conversationalist *Leskenoi* of modern times prevails.

"In Cold Hell, in Thicket" thematizes the distance itself. This distance is built of abstractions and boundaries, and can only be bridged by man raised through creativity commended by the environment. "The Moon Is the Number 18" speaks of yet other kinds of separations: those between the living and the dead, creatures hosted by the red tower and the blue moon, approached through Catholicism and sorcery. "To Gerhardt" is the last old poem to be incorporated from the volume *In Cold Hell, in Thicket.* In the new context concerning distances, it reveals new preoccupations: with splits between cultures and continents, past and present, with displacement and ways of healing this displacement, especially the mythological sources connecting one to land, space, and locality.

These are the ten poems that form the first half of the volume, providing a foundation to build on with other versions of distances and removals, as well as possibilities for bridging. Olson obeys his internal routes in a projective way, thus recharging mental and linguistic energies that might reduce barriers and separations. Robert J. Bertholf sees a "grand design" [13] in the architecture of the whole volume as the poems of the two halves interact with each other in the larger field of composition. Together, they express Olson's "stay against confusion," and articulate his distances and isolation from the world, as well as connections between self and experience.

A cluster of three historical poems comes at the beginning of the new section of the volume. "Letter for Melville 1951" is a bitter attack on the academic or professional separation that Olson sensed in the scholarly world of literature. The event that occasioned the poem was the Melville Society's "One Hundredth Birthday Party" for *Moby Dick,* held in September 1951. Olson published it as a broadside, a fold-out book, or object, that stood out as an alien product in the world of academia. As John Wieners remembered, "This piece was written in a 'moment of flame' at the end of August, 1951, as a bit of 'verse pamphleteering.' The students at Black Mountain College were so excited by the poem that they raised enough money among themselves to get it printed so that it might be sold at the birthday celebration which it attacks"

(Charters, 78). The poem's point of attack is exactly that separation and distance that Olson saw between Melville himself and academic Melville scholars—this "bunch of commercial travellers" who seem to use Melville for their own vulgar purposes, only to "scratch each other's backs with a dead man's hand."

The scholars are attacked for their lack of intuitive comprehension and animation, for being unable (and unwilling) to get emotionally involved with their subject. Wanting so much to comfortably "avoid the traffic," they "avoid" Melville, too: "Timed in such a way to avoid him, to see / he gets a lot of lip (who hung in a huge jaw) / and no service at all." To such banquets Melville will not come, Olson insists, because there "the arrowhead of his attention, / the accurate way he said the simple things, is not appreciated. He shall not visit those who miss typewriter altars in a tree." For Olson, Melville's major lesson centered on space: projective space of kinetic processes registered by perceptions. The poem closes with the image of such projective space completely missed by Melville critics:

> who does not know that it is not the point
> either of the hook or the plume which lies
> cut on this brave man's grave
> —on all of us—
> but that where they cross in motion,
> where they constantly moving cross anew, cut
> this new instant open—as he is who
> it this weekend in his old place
> presume on

The reader of Melville first has to understand the kind of consciousness *Moby Dick* presents: Ahab's and Ishamel's, as Olson expounded upon their difference in *Call Me Ishmael*. Ahab's conquering overlordship, with its appetite and obsession, misses the reality of space and nature in the same way Melville critics miss Melville by their abstract discourse and alienating approach. Ishmael, however, out of ecological obedience, is capable of grasping the tumultuous density of American space, this ever-changing, growing, animated, vital force.

The American Civil War is the thematic territory of "Anecdotes of the Late War." Olson takes the Civil War as the shameful lowest point, "the basement," in American history, the time when the whole land became infected with pejorocracy embodied by the greed for land, or "real estate." The poem claims, Bertholf observes, that "the Civil War forced pollution and corruption on the land and on the history of the nation." The Civil War is portrayed here as a distancing event that removed the nation "one step further from the vitality of the geography of the country" (Bertholf, 24).

The voice and persona of Mencius, the Chinese Confucian philosopher, is used in the next poem which discusses the distances modern economy has created in society. "I, Mencius, Pupil of the Master" recalls the way industry (iron/steel) as a force counteracts poetry and philosophy in ancient China as well as in modern America (Pittsburgh), mocking old virtues like equity and integrity, and replacing them with whorehouses and slums.

> when iron (steel)
> has expelled Confucius
> from China. Pittsburgh!
> beware: the Master
> betrays his vertu.

The speaking voice of the poem is aware of the duty of poets and artists: "at this hour / open galleries. And sell / Chinese prints." As the "pupil of the master," he is also aware of the responsibility of art at this time of consumerism and mercantilism: "no line must sleep, / that as the line goes so goes / the Nation!" This is a dictum clearly echoing Pound, who wrote in his *ABC of Reading* that "A people that grows accustomed to sloppy writing is a people in process of losing grip on its empire and on itself."[14] The poet's job, then, is to "keep his trade" in spite of the corruption and pollution, the separations and distances:

> We still look
>   and see
>   what we see
>   We do not see
>   ballads
> other than our own.

The death poem that follows seems to speak of different kinds of separations: those between cultures, continents, civilizations, and that break that death brings between kindred spirits like Olson and Gerhardt. For in the poem entitled "The Death of Europe" Olson mourns the death at age 28 of his young German friend Rainer M. Gerhardt. The poem celebrates the friendship of the man who gave Olson and Creeley "hearing / in Germany," a poet of Dionysian spirit, with whom he shared an assessment of the possibilities of human knowledge.

> It is not hell you came into,
> or came out of. It is not moly
> any of us are given. It is merely
> that we are possessed of
> the irascible. We are blind
> not from the darkness
> but by creation we are
> moles. We are let out
> sightless, and thus miss
> what we are given,

The poem acknowledges the finality of death: Olson offers laurels and flowers as memorials, and throws dirt into the grave. With the same gesture, however, he turns to man's duty on earth: the gaining of knowledge from that ground in which the dead are buried and the living are planted, so that the ground becomes the sky arching above the earth. "Let us who live / try."

Side by side with this total acknowledgment of death, we find poems expressing Olson's conviction about the dead living on in the minds of the living. "You live with your people as well as your ghosts," he once said in an interview; "you gotta live with them" (*Muthologos,* 1:172). Toward the end of the *The Distances,* there is a cluster of dream, nightmare, or death poems, of which "The Death of Europe" is the first. "A Newly Discovered 'Homeric' Hymn," "As the Dead Prey upon Us," "The Lordly and Isolate Satyrs," "The Librarian," and "Moonset, Gloucester, December 1, 1957, 1:58 A.M." belong here, all of them touching upon the distances that the various forms of consciousness create.

"A Newly Discovered 'Homeric' Hymn" speaks of the unbridgeable gap between the living and the dead, between normal and "altered" states of consciousness. The figures of the dead melt into those who are drunk or who have touched the pot:

> Hail
> and beware of the earth, where the dead come from. Life
> is not of the earth. The dead are of the earth. Hail and beware
> the earth, where the pot is buried.

The earth seems to embody that complex and contradictory relationship to death that Olson already touched upon in "The Death of Europe"; the acts of burial and planting both use the earth as ground, as the place where grounding is possible. These otherworldly creatures seem to possess some wisdom that is unattainable for the living, yet at the same time essential for them too:

> Hail and beware them, for they come from where you have not been,
> they come from where you cannot have come, they come into life
> by a different gate. They come from a place which is not easily known,
> it is known only to those who have died.
>
> . . . .
>
> Hail and beware them, in their season. Take care. Prepare
> to receive them, they carry what the living cannot do without,

Similarly mysterious otherworldly creatures appear in "The Lordly and Isolate Satyrs." In Olson's vision motorcyclists on the beach turn into Dionysian satyrs, expanding the consciousness of the viewer and initiating a revelatory experience. The motorcyclists appear as boddisatvahs, Buddhist deities of "monumental solidity," with weight and separateness, as gods, "the Androgynes," "the Great Halves." Actually, they turn out to be "the Contemporaries" who, with their "immensities," occupy the landscape but open it at the same time:

> . . . they are the unadmitted, the club of Themselves,
> weary riders, but who sit upon the landscape as the Great
> Stones. And only have fun among themselves. They are
> the lonely ones

Their presence reveals new areas on the beach, new vistas in the landscape: they create "the beach we had not known was there." "Every- / thing opened," the poem insists; "they have given us a whole new half of beach." A peculiar intensity of vision characterizes this satyr-poem, a vision permeated by love and alertness that makes life complete in the same manner as the satyrs complete the beach. These inaccessible and solid creatures propose the lesson: reconnect with nature, if only through the brilliance and splendour of death. "And winter's ice shall be as brilliant in its time as / life truly is, as Nature is only the offerer, and it is we / who look to see what the beauty is."

Inner and outer landscape, the dead and the living melt into each other in the elegy "As the Dead Prey upon Us." The poem dramatizes

the ways by which we have to live with our ghosts, "the dead in
ourselves," who blatantly ignore boundaries. The inner landscape is
populated with figures from Olson's childhood, now living in his memory and imagination. It is especially his mother who insistently returns:

> I found out she returns to the house once a week, and with her
> the throng of the unknown young who center on her as much in death
> as other like suited and dressed people did in life

The visitation of the dead seems to help the poet see clearly those nets
of being whose disentanglement is our ultimate task in life. Eternity
proves to be a false consolation: the demons remain, while the living are
captured in the multiple nets.—"The death in life (death itself) is
endless, eternity / is the false cause." The nets entangling us give
release and freedom from the weight of the demons only when the knots
catch fire and burn; but "[p]urity / is only an instant of being," to be
fought at every knot. All the five "hindrances" of Buddhism need to be
fought instant to instant in order to achieve perfection, purity and
finally release:

> O souls, burn
> alive, burn now
>
> that you may forever
> have peace,
>
> . . . .
> And if she sits in happiness the souls
> who trouble her and me
> will also rest.

A struggle for release from the oppressive and inhibiting presence of
the dead mother permeates the poem "Moonset, Gloucester, December
1, 1957, 1:58 A.M." Here a rite is performed: in the form of a painful
exorcism the son is freeing himself forever from the overpowering
authority of the mother:

> . . . Rise
> Mother from off me
> God damn you God damn me my
> misunderstanding of you
>
> I can die now I just begun to live

A similarly powerful inner drama is captured in "The Librarian," a deeply personal poem treating distances between interior and exterior events. "The best poem I ever wrote," Olson said of "The Librarian" (*Muthologos* 1:171); indeed, it deals with later preoccupations like Gloucester as psychic landscape and the persona of Maximus. Descending in his mind into Gloucester, the poet is confronted with a flood of ghosts and memories that make up the landscape: "The landscape (the landscape!) again: Gloucester, / the shore one of me is (duplicates), and from which / (from offshore, I, Maximus) am removed, Observe." The landscape—in Sherman Paul's sense of "the field defined by the limits of a single view (single self)" (Paul, 122)—is inner and outer at the same time. Populated by duplicates belonging to both worlds, the exterior landscape is presented here as it is internalized, or, more precisely, both as the product of internalization and in the process of being internalized. The poem, as Hallberg claims, "is set in a 'Black Space,' a nightmare landscape occupied by not wholly imaginary phantoms— yet it's Gloucester too (von Hallberg 1978, 88). The father turning into the librarian, Frank Moore melting into the figure of Olson's brother "that got born misshapen" (*Muthologos* 1:169), the figures appearing at the poetry reading, Olson's daughter and first wife—these are all persona with "duplicates" in the interior landscape, exposing psychic distances to be bridged. Their existence is made real in the interior geography: "I have moved them in, to my country."

We experience here, as Hallberg puts it, "Gloucester climbing down into Olson's mind: the librarian, keeper of the records, has been intimate with Olson's former wife in his parents' bedroom; the poet's subject matter has come to life and invaded his psychic sanctuaries" (Hallberg, 89). The distances that are articulated in the poem are manifold: between the material from poetry and personal memory, "the shore one of me" and the "offshore," the out-of-reach and the interiorized, the duplicates come together into figures like father/son, father/daughter, husband/wife, brother/friend, man/art, Maximus/city.

Locality, the spirit or power of place, offers a way for bridging these distances, provides the sense of being grounded: "I am caught / in Gloucester." Gloucester is the place and a power to be obeyed; only as such is it capable of holding Olson-Maximus and Frank Moore, "that damned fuckin' doppelganger . . . of *me*" (*Muthologos* 1:172), in one unit, as well as buried and hidden realities and dark events. In the following passage Creeley writes about Olson's sense of location and geography in these poems:

The poems themselves are, then, the issue of an engagement, of an impinge-
ment, a location that is constantly occurring. They are not a decision of forms
more than such forms may be apprehended, literally gained, as possible in the
actual writing. "But a field / is not a choice . . .," however much within it
may occur that sense of "choice" he takes care to qualify as *recognition*. It is in
this sense that Olson has been *given* Gloucester, . . . It is how Olson is
involved with this place, that is interesting, how it is that he is "caught in
Gloucester." (*A Quick Glance,* 177)

"Variations Done for Gerald Van De Wiele" and "The Distances"
bring the volume to its close by speaking of other ways of bridging
and healing: an elemental coincident relationship with nature through
intense experience and the power of love bringing objects of art to
life.

The life-giving gesture of art as a way "to undo distance" is treated in
"The Distances." In the field of the poem the figures of Zeus and
Augustus, Pygmalion and Galatea, and the German inventor Karl
Tanzler and his Cuban lover all occur to point at the possibilities for
drawing connections between art and life, self and world. Pygmalion's
love for his statue brings it to life as Galatea; in the same way Tanzler
keeps the dead body of his lover in his bed as if she were alive. But what
Tanzler cannot accomplish with the help of science, Pygmalion does
achieve through art.

>   Death is a loving matter, then, a horror
>   we cannot bide, and avoid
>   by greedy life
>   we think all living things are precious
>   —Pygmalions

"Mastery" and control seem to be forces contrary to love: old Zeus, like
the 83-year-old X-ray technician, "a god throned on torsoes," is governed by his greed, and cannot offer much to the younger as a teaching,
although: "Sons go there hopefully as though there was a secret, the
object / to undo distance?" Opposed to this masterly love fed by greed
and the desire to control, Olson offers the force that truly has the power
to heal and undo the distances: a love as obedient as art and poetry are.
The volume closes with Aphrodite's imperative that brings Galatea to
life.

O love who places all where each is, as they are, for every moment,
yield
   to this man
that the impossible distance
be healed,
   that young Augustus
   and old Zeus
be enclosed

   "I wake you,
stone. Love this man."

"Variations Done for Gerald Van De Wiele" "Variations Done for Gerald Van De Wiele" is a complex poem written during the spring of 1956, toward the end of Olson's Black Mountain period. Gerry Van De Wiele was an art student at the college, and the poem dedicated to him carries unmistakable signs of the Black Mountain spirit and philosophy. It is composed in three parts, three movements each expressing a different variation on the theme of the possible unity of man and nature, body and soul. The poem is a variation on Rimbaud's poem entitled "O saisons, ô châteaux," which initial inspiration is easily traced in the incorporation of French lines as well as Olson's own translations weaving through the poem. The thesis-antithesis-synthesis structure takes the form, as Charles Altieri puts it, of the romantic triad of innocence, experience, and higher innocence[15] or of the triple approach of observation-argument-action. What is being treated in a complex manner is the ultimate human condition as embodied in the conflict between displacement in nature versus participation and unity. The distances that the whole volume is dedicated to are given a grand dramatization here.

The first section bears the French title "Le Bonheur," a word borrowed from the original Rimbaud poem: "Happiness," is the ultimate goal to be pursued and attained in life. It starts out with a series of observations about emerging spring, a scene of turmoil and energy presented in short, intensive images.

      dogwood flakes
      what is green

      the petals
      from the apple
      blow on the road

> mourning doves
> mark the sway
> of the afternoon, bees
> dig the plum blossoms
>
> the morning
> stands up straight, the night
> is blue from the full of April moon

All five verbs of these opening lines refer to some specific action characterized by a marked directionality: *flakes, blow, mark, dig, stands up.*
What is common to all these verbs is the feature of expressing vigor,
energy, drive, and arrowlike motion—all that, according to Olson,
creates the natural context for man, who might use it as a source from
which to derive his own energy. Indeed, Olson's attention turns now to
man's place in this spring turmoil, and his possibilities for participation. He likens himself to the Diesel and the whippoorwill, both
disrupting the natural cycle: "no other birds but us / are as busy." Here
the poem gets more abstract as we follow him struggling with his
intellect and attention to realize his likeness and difference.

> (O saisons, ô châteaux!
> Délires!
>
> What soul
> is without fault?
>
> Nobody studies
> happiness
>
> Every time the cock crows
> I salute him
>
> I have no longer any excuse
> for envy. My life
>
> has been given its orders: the seasons
> seize
>
> the soul and the body, and make mock
> of any dispersed effort. The hour of death
>
> is the only trespass

This whole passage is Olson's translation, or, to be more exact, his adaptation with variation of Rimbaud's original. A more exact translation would read:

> Oh seasons, oh castles,
> What soul is without fault?
>
> Oh seasons, oh castles,
>
> I did the magic study
> Of happiness, which eludes no one.
>
> Oh, long live happiness, each
> time its Gallic cock crows.
>
> I shall have no envy,
> It has taken charge of my life.
>
> This charm! It took my soul and body
> and dispersed all efforts.
>
> How are my words to be understood
> It [happiness] makes my words flee and fly!

For Rimbaud, the castles with their towers are loaded with phallic associations; for Olson, however, they turn into images of permanence and the human possibility for being grounded in earth. In the original, no metaphysical dimensions are involved. Happiness taking charge of the poet's life is directly related to the proud Gallic cock, an image heavy with priapic implications. In Olson's version, however, it is the seasons, the natural cycle, that seize the soul and the body, and it is death that brings about the flight. Olson's crowing cock is primarily related to this natural cycle, having Biblical rather than sexual overtones (especially since the scene take place in "the full of April moon," that is, at Easter). At this point the recollecting consciousness is faced with the impossibility of full participation: man is both removed from the natural cycle and is part of it at the same time. The unpunctuated text leaves the end unresolved.

Section 2 returns to the simple observations of the first movement without the sense that this multitude or multiplicity is unified or coordinated by some immanent law: all becomes scattered and dis-

persed as the day progresses. In a paradoxical way, separateness and
union both permeate the scene; the poet is participating in both, being
busy unlike most other creatures but at the same time conversing with
the moon. The participation turns into a conscious effort now, in the
form of the study of happiness.

> what soul
> isn't in default?
>
> can you afford not to make
> the magical study
> which happiness is

This section states the philosophical and ethical argument of the poem,
as "being without fault" grows into the state of "being in default," the
failure to fullfil an obligation or the avoidance of the charge.

> do you know the charge,
>
> that you shall have no envy, that your life
> has its orders, that the seasons
>
> seize you too, that no body and soul are one
> if they are not wrought
>
> in this retort?

The charge appears here in its double sense of burden/task and source of
energy/reward, and the effort of the active study of happiness, "retort,"
is what reconciles the two senses of "charge" as well as body and soul.
This retort is much like the concept of feedback: human action responding to the laws and orders in nature, and thus returning the charge so
that death can be affirmed at the close of the section.

The final part of the poem brings synthesis to the argument. Section
3, "Spring," seems to roar with action, with the dogwood lighting up
the day, the moon flaking the night, birds being a multiude, flowers
ravined by bees, blossoms thrown to the ground, and the wind and rain
forcing everything. Altieri points to the "active role of the body," the
"unifying sexual power of the generalized forces of wind and rain," and
"a hymn of sexual verbs embodying the union of natural energy, body,
and consciousness" in this section (*ET,* 106).

> even the night is drummed
> by whippoorwills, and we get
>
> as busy, we plow, we move,
> we break out, we love. The secret
> which got lost neither hides
> nor reveals itself, it shows forth
>
> tokens.

Only fragments are revealed in this vision. More and more, spring becomes acceptance, engagement and devotion to one's responsibility, and participation in its transmutations. Singleness and totality permeate the picture; death is of no concern.

> the matutinal cock clangs
> and singleness: we salute you
>
> season of no bungling

This is a difficult and complicated poem, both philosophically and poetically. As an open field poem, it invites a process of interpretations, of which the above short sketch is only a start.

Five

The Maximus Poems

However hopeless it may seem, we have no other choice: we must
go back to the beginning.

—William Carlos Williams

The Maximus Poems, a monumental masterwork, crowns Charles Olson's
poetic achievement. It is an immense book, consisting of 300 poems
written over a period of 20 years. Volume 1, *The Maximus Poems,* was
published in 1960, *Maximus Poems IV, V, VI* in 1968, while the last
book, *The Maximus Poems: Volume Three* came out after Olson's death, in
1975. The whole is now available in a single volume, due to the heroic
effort of the late Charles Butterick. It is, as Michael Davidson points
out, "possessed of a size and weight of other books (*The Divine Comedy,*
the Bible, the OED) that could be said to contain at least a modicum of
'earthly existence.' " It is indeed a weighty book, whose "sheer bulk
(8 ½ × 11 ½ × 2) replicates its scope, if not its author's size,"
Davidson goes on.[1]

Maximus is a book-length poem composed of autonomous individual
pieces. It belongs to the tradition of the American "long poem," the
modern poetic sequence whose roots reach back to Walt Whitman and
Leaves of Grass. Whitman provided a model for the modern poetic
treatment of history, where individual lyric pieces achieve epic dimension when placed in relationship to each other in a single lifetime work.
Olson's modern American epic is a nonnarrative poem composed of
heterogeneous poetic materials; its autonomous individual pieces do
not follow a linear sequence, but instead are characterized by a fragmented succession of heights of poetic intensities. Like his predecessors
in the American epic tradition, Olson attempted to capture the wholeness of life—but he left his readers with the responsibility of recon-
structing wholeness and unity from his open postmodern text. *Maximus*
is permeated with Olson's "curriculum and practice of history," where
the reader becomes, as Davidson observes, "an archeologist among
undecoded glyphs" (Davidson, 189). More importantly, *Maximus* relates an inward journey, a process of revelation, "his-story," that of

Jung's "individuated man," who, in Sherman Paul's words, "has real-ized the self, who, having reconciled the opposites of his nature, is whole" (Paul, 118).

Loaded with references—historical, scientific, mythological, per-sonal—*Maximus* is a most difficult poem. George Butterick's *Guide to "The Maximus Poems"* is perhaps longer than the book it tries to explain. This long postmodern epic though seemingly fragmented, moves in concentric circles, returning to the same themes, images, names, references again and again throughout the nine books of the three volumes. Merrill speaks of "parallel concerns": "the epic rarely proceeds in straight lines but rather moves in spirals, picking up subjects and themes again and again, each time from a somewhat different approach" (Merrill, 177). Olson, however, rejected Paul Blackburn's remark that he was going around the subject, "He sd, 'You go all around the subject.' And I sd, 'I didn't know it was / a subject.' He sd, 'You twist' and I sd 'do' " ("Maximus, to Gloucester, Letter 15").

Origins

The American long poems created by Whitman, Pound, Williams, Crane, Zukofsky, Olson, Duncan, and others are open-ended, lacking any preconceived compositional pattern. They have no overall "story," no consistent meter, no recurring structure, no finish or closure. Writ-ten over a lifetime, these poems end only when their authors die and stop adding to them. *Maximus* is permeated by Olson's attitude of "I can't 'finish the song' " (*Muthologos,* 2:82); though always a work-in-progress, it develops flexible and open formal strategies that prevent it from being nothing more than a massive poetic fragment. An overall epic unity is gained, for example, by the epistolary form that more or less dominates the text, by the person of Maximus, the narrator, and the locality, Gloucester, and also by the author's consistent moral com-mitment that holds the poem's teachings together in spite of the pro-gressively expanding world the poem creates. Yet nowhere does the poem strive to achieve completeness; it is a process poem, where forces such as historical facts, dreams, and stories from the collective memory of the community simultaneously generate the *field* of the poem.

The origins of the poem go back to the late 1940s, to a proposal Olson drafted after withdrawing from politics. According to Butterick, he first had in mind a poem entitled *WEST* that would have covered "the history of Western man for the past 2,500 years." This proposal was soon modified into "a planned book of narratives which Olson tentatively titled *Red, White & Black,*" offering a morphology of American culture from the earliest times.[2] The point, according to Butterick, would have been what Olson called the "saturation job" in "A Bibliography on America": "The job is, by the techniques of total research, to track down any events or person so completely that you can, in the minutiae of the facts, find the elements of which the event or person are made and which make them significant to other men" (Butterick 1978, xxii). Indeed, *Maximus* is the product of such a saturation job, built on a foundation of philological and scholarly research, as well as moral commitment.

Basically, two constant elements in this majestic long poem contribute to its textual solidity: place and hero. *Maximus* is centered upon one place, the city of Gloucester, Massachusetts, with whose "psychic and material contours" we become intimately familiar.[3] For both poet and reader Gloucester is transformed into a sacred, magical place, "one of the holy places in this world," in Duncan's words, where the since lost coincidence of man and *locus* can be still traced.[4] Olson's idea of the long poem owes much to Pound and Williams, as many critics would agree; however, the way Gloucester acts as microcosm (the local opening into the universal) in *Maximus* makes mock of the label "derivative." It fulfills its grand ambition by focusing, as Butterick observes, "on a single locality that serves as a microcosm by which to measure the present and the nation and which grows to encompass earth, heaven, and hell" (Butterick 1978, xix).

In another sense, though, Gloucester as place seems indeed arbitrary, chosen, as Don Byrd observes, perhaps for no other reason than the happy summers Olson spent there as a child."[5] According to Byrd, the center of the poem "is not a place as such but an engagement of attentions which is necessarily *located*" (Byrd, 64).

Moreover, in *Maximus* hero and locality come together exactly by this *engagement of attentions:* Maximus is a "root person" anchored in a "root city" in a way probably inspired by Williams, whose *Paterson* was one of Olson's models. But while Paterson the man is related to Paterson the city in a metaphorical way, Maximus is part of Gloucester metonymically, by history and topography. In Eshleman's words, a "congruence of man and earth" is embodied in the Maximus-Gloucester relationship (Eshleman MS).

Maximus of Gloucester has his metaphorical ties, too, to Maximus of

Tyre, a second century Neoplatonic philosopher, whom Olson discovered somewhat accidentally in 1949, while reading Greek poetry. This chance finding proved to be very fruitful; the historical Maximus's *Dissertations* might easily have determined some core ideas for Olson. The name proved to be most fitting for Olson (being the superlative of *big, great*); Olson exploits this meaning, and allows the metaphor of the name to come into being. As Byrd claims, "Maximus is proposed as a figure who is equal to the immense spaces and stretches of history that comprise the outward facts of his existence. He is an image of possibilities inherent in that situation" (Byrd, 55). Correspondences between Olson and the Neoplatonic philosopher relating to locus as well as teaching are also important. Tyre and Gloucester, seaports on the Mediterranian and Atlantic respectively, played a crucial role in the history of their regions, and at the same time cradled communities that fell from grace into corruption. Maximus of Tyre was a teacher on the move—much like Olson. His teachings concern possible human communities, based especially on the criterion of man's cooperation with or exploitation of nature. Frank Davey convincingly shows that Olson could have found inspirations for his ideas on greed, pride, ambition, and man living off nature in Maximus's *Dissertations*. Olson was most probably reassured in his convictions by the tenets he found in *Dissertations,* especially by those referring to obedience, cooperation with nature, respect for the integrity of all living beings, including domesticated animals, and the possibility of building a *polis* where control, imposition, and exploitation are unknown human forces (see especially Davey, 291–97).

The same structural principle, or rather the lack of it, pervades the whole poem. Much like with abstract expressionist or action painting, the making and the process outweigh in importance the product, the thing made. "In this aesthetic," Robert Duncan explains, "conception cannot be abstracted from doing; beauty is related to the beauty of an archer hitting the mark. Referred to its source in the act, the intellect actually manifest as energy, as presence is doing, is the measure of our *arêtê* (as vision, claritas, light, illumination, was the measure of Medieval *arêtê*)."[6] Indeed, *Maximus* is a process poem in the sense that it faithfully follows the process of reality and creation without falling prey to the interfering constraint of the creative ego. The creative faculty active in the writing of the poem is not control but attention and listening, or letting go, letting form take care of itself; the poet, according to this poetics, follows forces outside himself while he is

submerged in the process of intensive perception. Thus *Maximus* becomes the ultimate projectivist poem, where one perception follows the
other without the interposition of creative will.

The process of the poem can best be captured by the term Frank
Davey uses: "natural unfolding" or "unfolding form," that is, the natural process during which "the essential reality and process which is
being hidden from man must be attended to, must be heard" (Davey,
298). This process of natural unfolding accounts for some of the difficulties in comprehending the poem: Olson demands an active alertness
from the reader who is perhaps used to the more traditional passive
interpreter's role. What Olson demands of the reader is that he/she be
constantly in a state of perceptual alertness, constantly curbing his/her
urge for easy readings and final interpretive solutions. The field is
open, energy is free to flow, no terminus puts barriers on the flow of
writing.

Clayton Eshleman points to this open-ended, nonconclusive nature
of *The Maximus Poems* as the most significant trait of the exciting new
poetry emerging in the 1960s; this new poetry was discontinuous and
resembled a "spill of water," with "its content determining its form,
each poem responsible to the energy it tapped in the process of being
written out." What Eshleman finds packed in Olson's *Maximus* is "a
mind in ceaseless inquiry and self-scrutiny which preferred the probe to
the synthesis." This poetry demands total involvement from the reader
because "the fragment or the fragments offer imaginative space for the
reader to fill in, to draw mental lines from node to node and thus to
constellate his own perspective" (Eshleman MS).

Olson's demand that poetry be true to the processes of reality also lies
at the bottom of his urge to be precise and exact. Seeking always for the
right word, he wishes to recover the primordial integrity of language,
where words act as objects, basic realities, with one-to-one verbal correspondences. "There may be no more names than there are objects /
There can be no more verbs than there are actions," he writes in "Tyrian
Businesses," propagating the ideal of austerity as opposed to abundance
in the field of linguistic expression. He wishes to use a "particularizing
vocabulary,"[7] one that would give an "exacting registration" and "the
most acute possible measurement"[8] for life's processes. "Nowhere is
there room for carelessness," Olson states ("Letter 7"). Expressions of
this compulsion to tell the truth weave through the long poem; Olson-
Maximus considers it a commitment, a mission, to be always accurate,

to be true to facts, to get it straight. As the motto introducing book 3 of volume 1 says,

> On ne doit aux morts nothing
> else than
> la vérité

Taken from Voltaire via an essay on Cabot, the original French lines translate as: "One owes respect to the living; one owes the dead only the truth."

Thematic Elements

Sherman Paul points to several binary thematic elements in *Maximus:* sea vs. land, outward vs. inward, fishing (and poetry) vs. capitalism (slavery, advertising), polis vs. pejorocracy, local vs. absentee landlords, care vs. carelessness, work vs. sloth. These values are expressed by images drawing on sight, smell, and hearing (Paul, 130). Maximus teaches his readers sensual and perceptual awareness.

The *polis* vs. *pejorocracy* problem is a major theme that runs through *The Maximus Poems* in many forms and variations. It connects several of the opposites, and expresses Olson's concept of the "moral struggle" of American history "Because of the agora America is, was, from the start, the moral struggle" ("Maximus, to Himself, Letter 14"). "Finding out for himself," Olson digs deep into historical documents to show the corruption that mercantilism and the exploitation of nature and man has brought upon America. By showing the struggle between "individual right to subsist in one's context and exploitative ambitions of large institutions" (Davey, 305), Olson's poetry becomes a moral statement teaching the primeval integrity and posture that the "first comers" knew but the power-seeking "second comers" forgot. Being a "professor of posture" in a world whose mercantile value system mocks first-comer values, Olson is not shy about his intention to teach, to radically change minds and convert souls. He does this by making, as Merrill puts it, *polis,* the community, "the moral center of gravity of *The Maximus Poems,*" *polis* being a nucleus of true believers, an ideal, an obedience, "an integrity and prime of value" (Merrill, 173).

Von Hallberg points out the fact that polis as city "has nothing directly to do with a large number of people living in a relatively small area of place," and insists on defining polis as "the quality of the relationships between people" (von Hallberg 1978, 56). When Olson finally found his "trade," his "business," it turned out to be related exactly to this quality between people; as L. S. Dembo puts it, "Maximus' 'trade' (and therefore his identity) is the reconstruction of polis with the tools of language or, in practical terms, the articulation of a vision of man's moral history and fate."[9]

The quality of relationships between polis people is characterized by attention, care, and a pervading morality of perception. Clear perception governs the clarity of the "coming in"—through the eye and the ear and the mind (see "The Songs of Maximus, Song 1"); but attention and care are twofold: the "going out" is also a moral issue for polis people when the demand to respond is emphasized. As Duncan puts it, the "discipline of the eye" is coupled with "a speech in which the eye works" (Duncan, 189), the law of *perception* with the necessity of *response*.

"Self-things" and "self-acts" are part of this idea of polis, being defined by participation and immanence. Self-things, with their self-existence, are charged by that active, obeying relationship to their context. Thus, *Maximus* is full of such "self-things": the tansy, the nest-building bird, the fishermen of Gloucester, the seventeenth-century carpenter, Captain John Smith, the Lady of Good Voyage, Gloucester itself at one time, and, of course, Maximus himself. All these self-things are useless from the world's point of view because they earn no measurable gain or profit for themselves. Their struggle is measured by self-rewarding gratitude and authenticity, and not by worldly success. Thus these self-things become marginal by social measures, but retain their autonomy as outsiders—much the same way as Olson himself wanted to remain an outsider, being aware of the multiple gains of this status. As Clayton Eshleman aptly puts it, "an independent intellectual, on the periphery of mainstream activity, he had the advantages of one situated at the boundaries." As Eshleman argues, Olson also knew that: "great art, with occasional exceptions, is always peripheral, for if it had genuine size it is too evocative of the cosmic instability that especially now has moved into the foreground of our daily existence" (Eshleman MS).

The Maximus Poems, Letters 1–10

Letters 1–10 were first published by Jonathan Williams in 1953 in his Jargon series, to be followed by *The Maximus Poems/11–22* in 1956.

The complete first triad, that is, volume 1, became in 1960 a joint Jargon-Corinth project entitled *The Maximus Poems*. The units of this triad were not numbered, although the sections were quite clear from the succession of publishing dates. Bit by bit, branch by branch, *Maximus* grew organically, each poem appearing in the order of its writing. Olson had no overall structure in mind while arranging the individual poems, but instead played it "by ear."

However, the texture of the volume is thoroughly interwoven. Images related to building and creation, a series of "familiar" objects man has become estranged from, the drama of heroes and villains in Gloucester's history, recurring archival records and personal-biographical materials, the "practice of the self," the turnings of human attitudes—these are poetic components that are present in each spill of water that this long poem is, granting identifiable substance to each particle: the *Maximus*-substance.

The first poem, "I, Maximus of Gloucester, to You," which Olson called "a classic invocation of the muse" (*Muthologos,* 2:82), already contains many of these poetic molecules. The poet makes plain the task he is undertaking: to set out on a quest, on a voyage, a "forwarding," in search of something that might be the commonest thing. He is concerned, as Byrd puts it, for "the *quantity* of attention which experience receives," and directs attention to the possibilities of "a coincidence of consciousness and space" (Byrd, 67): "the thing you're after may lie around the bend or the nest." The gentle steep roofs and the statue of the Lady of Good Voyage evoke the poet's expression of his love for his city, but also compel him to recognize the corrupting commodities of Gloucester pejorocracy: the spray-gunned billboards, the neon advertisments, the waxlike figures attentionless of the "demand," the "mu-sick" of the jukebox, and other cheap entertainment. But, he insists, "The fundament / still your own" ("Maximus, to Gloucester, Letter 14"). In quest for "that which matters, that which insists, that which will last," in search of the "underpart" beneath oil-slicked surfaces, Maximus is driven by two opposing forces: rage and love, destruction and construction. He is the blacksmith of the metal-hot lance to be used in both battle and fishing (cf. the swordsman striking the blue-red back of the swordfish), preparing him for his difficult mission. Fish imagery runs through the whole poem, evoking both the origin of the seaport settlement and the archetypal symbol of Christianity, of abundance and regeneration, of life and fertility. In Maximus's view, fish granted a morally acceptable existence to the fishing communities of the Atlantic for centuries, helping them to retain their integrity by providing sustenance, not gain and profit out of the sea. Maximus digs into "the underpart" in search of this original condition. His rage and preparation for battle are complemented by the emphatic expression of the creative spirit: the nesting bird in the process of collecting material for (her?) nest, and binding it all together by love, "feather to feather added"—

> one loves only form
> and form only comes
> into existence when
> the thing is born

>> born of yourself, born
>> of hay and cotton struts,
>> of street pickings, wharves, weeds
>> you carry in, my bird

>>> of a bone of a fish
>>> of a straw, or will
>>> of a color, of a bell
>>> of yourself, torn

The urge to clean or even purge the city of "mu-sick," of pejorocracy, is just as strong in these poems as the ambition to reconstruct the older polis out of facts and records. The Lady of Good Voyage portrayed in "Letter 2" seems to offer a secure point of reference: she "has got it straight," standing in the midst of the "elements." But others in Gloucester also obeyed the commands of the elements. Maximus relates stories: of Howard Blackburn, who survived a storm by purposely allowing his hand to freeze to the oars; of Lou Douglas, Olson's neighbor, "the top of whose head a bollard clean took away"; of Frank Miles, who rescued two men in a storm one night, swimming them to shore; of Carl Olsen, who swam three miles with the dead body of his mate to find their vessel. All this is polis attitude, according to Maximus, and shows as a "demand" on faces and in eyes. According to Olson's radical statement, "polis is / eyes."

"Letter 3" mixes the softly lyric and the militant elements in a way similar to how the flower called tansy contains healing and destroying power. This medicinal herb is evoked in the poem to eliminate the odors of mercantilism and pejorocracy: "Tansy for them, / tansy for

Gloucester to take the smell / of all owners." Maximus demands that
owners, "absentee-owners," leave Gloucester, where "the wondership
[is] stolen by, / ownership." The task of Maximus is to restore the
integrity of the place, to rebuild Gloucester into the "root city" it used
to be, upon the foundation of those few for whom polis still exists.

> o tansy city, root city
> let them not make you
> as the nation is
>
> . . . .
>
> . . . Polis now
> is a few, is a coherence not even yet anew

The next poem, "The Songs of Maximus," continues to elaborate on
the nature of "mu-sick": "dirty / postcard" and words "all over everything" express, for Maximus, the sense of numbness and carelessness
that permeates the city: all the senses, including attention, are
"greased / lulled."

> all
> wrong
> And I am asked—ask myself (I, too, covered
> with the gurry of it) where
> shall we go from here

Counting the troubles that go with ownership (like the leaking faucet,
nonfunctioning plumbing, and broken car), Maximus offers a strong
sermon against affluence and the bondage of property, evoking a
sixteenth-century English lyric he had learned in school. With the
much-quoted passage on voluntary poverty, Maximus reaches back to
preindustial, premercantile ideals of poverty, freedom, rootedness, and
coherence.

The sense of being culturally rooted in polis is treated in "Letter 5."
The poem is addressed to one-time friend Vincent Ferrini, to whom all
these first letters were originally directed. Olson blames Ferrini, editor
of the Gloucester-based literary magazine, *Four Winds,* for not making
the magazine an outlet of local expression, for ignoring Gloucester's
possibility for becoming "the absolute place and thing that's theirs"
(*Muthologos,* 1:95). Olson's authentic writing, rich with intimate fac-
tual knowledge of the place, stands against rootless writing:

> I do not know that Four Winds has a place
> or a sight in it
> in a city where highliners breed,
> if it is not as good as fish is
>
> .   .   .   .
>
> Nor assuage yrself I use the local as a stick to beat you. Such
> pages as you now have published twice, do not need one small
> Gloucester thing to be a Glucester magazine.

Maximus is quite harsh in his judgement on Ferrini: "You have had a
broken trip, Mr. Ferrini. And you should go hide in your cellar." The
poem, however, is itself a model of the kind of locality and rootedness
Maximus has in mind, of a magazine that "walked on those legs all live
things walk on, / their own." He harks "back to an older polis," and
gives familar details of Gloucester's history: of the Portuguese skipper,
of the cheating of the C&R Construction Company, of Captain John
Smith. "The very accusation," Dembo observes, "reveals Maximus'
intimate knowledge of the local life, a knowledge that is necessary to
the precision of authentic writing and to the maintenance of polis"
(Dembo, 282). Maximus identifies the "old measure of care," care and
attention to the real life of the community, as the essential editorial
principle.

Maximus is trying to come up with various recommendations concerning a possible midway meeting with Ferrini, but all the suggested
locations prove impossible, until the letter closes in bitter disappointment.

> It's no use.
> There is no place we can meet.
> You have left Gloucester.
> You are not there, you are anywhere
> where there are little magazines
> will publish you

Throughout these first letters we witness a panorama of the acts and
doings of Olson's "pantheon of heroes" (Merrill, 183). The builders of
the polis are opposed to the destroyers of the community spirit. The
Gloucester men listed in "Letter 2," for example, became heroes for
proving their willingness to cooperate with the elements. The destroyers include Moulton in "Tyrian Businesses," overloading his ship with
lumber, and thus risking the vessel out of mere personal greed. In

"Letter 7," we read of Marsden Hartley, the painter of Dogtown, Helen Stein, also a painter and friend of Olson, and the seventeenth-century carpenter William Stevens, who built ships in Gloucester—these figures are all praised for their obedience to inner and local forces, for their commitment to create as opposed to the desire to "just live off nature." In the same poem the list goes on to include more whimsical and odd characters such as Thomas Morton, banished by the Pilgrims and later by the authorities of the Massachusetts Bay Colony for his deviant behavior, as well as Pound, the "American savage," the true-eyed Verrocchio of Florence, the mysterious Al Gorman, a fish buyer in Gloucester, and Mason Andrews, the local street peddler. These are all authentic polis people for Maximus, with "polis / in their eye." Realizing "the necessities of the practice of the self," they are the "cracks" in the wood.

> How much the cracks matter, or seems in a ship, the absolutes
> of swelling (the mother), of weather (as even in machine parts,
> tolerance
>
> Only: no latitude, any more than any, elite. The exactness
> caulking, or "play," calls for, those
> millimeters
>
> No where in man is there room for carelessnesses.

Particularizing exactness and faithful obedience to inner demands are the marks of authentic character here; these are the polis virtues, the commitment of the few, often eccentric, artists and creators, those who participate in the creative processes. They are the workers and creators, using attention and care to make extensions of their own self.

> Eyes,
> & polis
> fishermen,
> & poets
>   or in every human head I've known is
>   busy
> both:
> the attention, and
> the care
>   .   .   .   .

so few
have the polis
in their eye

("Letter 6")

This select society of polis is made up of "self-things," possessing a
distinct center of gravity, a "felicity / resulting from life of activity in
accordance with" ("Tyrian Businesses")—in accordance with their inner
demand.

these things
which don't carry their end any further than
their reality in
themselves.

("Letter 9")

Self-things perform self-acts where the inner and the outer exist in
harmony. Olson's favorite example for this unity is the dance, an action
that embodies both the physical and the spiritual and also serves as the
model for the creative process of writing and thinking. Thus, the
"exercise" developed in "Tyrian Businesses" attempts to capture this
integrity of the physical and spiritual while learning "how to dance /
sitting down."

Maximus has a long list of self-things. John White, for example,
who organized the Dorchester Fishing Company, is praised in "Letter
10" for his understanding of nature: he realized that fish, not puritan-
ism, served as the founding pillar of these Atlantic settlements ("It was
fishing first"). Such "first comers" as John White, Roger Conant, Chris-
topher Levett, Captain John Smith, and Captain Hewes (leader of the
14 Dorchester fishermen) represent a pre-industrial morality and integrity lost since the destruction of localism. Opposed to them are Miles
Standish, the "Short Chimney" ("Letter 11"), the slave trader John
Hawkins, James Bryant Conant, president of Harvard University, John
Endecott, first governor of Massachusetts Bay Colony—these are makers of pejorocracy, the "merchandize men" making quick money, "the
conquistadors of my country" ("The Song and Dance Of"). In this
drama of heroes and villains, explorers are opposed to colonizers, participants to profit makers, obedience to exploitation, need to gain, polis
values to mercantile attitudes. Maximus's list is exhaustive; his argument grandly sweeping.

A recurring case for the opposition of polis integrity and pejorocratic corruption is the example of the 14 Dorchester fishermen, related in a series of poems starting with "Letter 23." These poems express Olson's "attempt to be completely careful about the facts" of history (*Mutho-logos*, 2:85), "looking / for oneself for the evidence" in a Herodotian way. "Fishing interests" and "covenental interests" clashed (Merrill, 186) when Miles Standish finally destroyed this small polis in the "Stage Fight." Olson praises these 14 men for their capacity for obedience and attention, for their courage for nakedness as a way to intensify perception and interchange.

> nakedness is what one means
> is what one means
>
> that all start up
> to the eye and soul
> as though it had never
> happened before
>   ("Maximus, to Gloucester")

It is the "sincere and desperate attention to the physical nature of man's conditions," as Davey points out, that draws Maximus's admiration for these men; "marooned in for a winter in a previously uninhabited wilderness, they took great care to harmonize themselves with the physical features of the landscape" (Davey, 303–4). These hardy Dorchester men could survive the New England winter because they had the capacity to perceive the place and act according to the demands they understood coming from locality: "they took their shelter either side of softer Stage Head and let / Tablet Rock buff for them the weather side." They even built a house that was to last for 300 years (to be hauled to Salem to satisfy the governor's greed). "Such participation with reality, such care to adapt, strikes Olson as indisputable proof that most of these fourteen men were real men with accurate eyes for what is important in nature," Davey states (Davey, 304). Finally these men became victims of the exploitative ambitions of the Puritans: they had to give way to Miles Standish and other attacking second comers. But Olson erects this poetic monument to their integrity.

According to Ed Dorn, "On first Looking Out through Juan de la Cosa's Eyes" is "the best single poem" of the *Maximus* sequence. "It has," he explains, "more exactly the particular turnings, springs, shutters, the weavings, and the riding away, that I take it this verse has when it works best" (Dorn, 305). The poem takes its materials from the adventures and diaries of the earliest explorers, the very "first comers" of the Atlantic, the Mediterranean, and the Phoenician Sea. Maximus's sources and references include Juan de la Cosa, Saint Brendan, fifteenth-century Breton fishermen, Homer, the discoverers of Newfoundland, Columbus, the *Titantic,* as well as Gloucester fishermen. Juan de la Cosa, whose eyes we are looking through, was Columbus's "chief chart maker," traveling with him as the captain of the *Nina;* he explored the West Indies, and became famous for drawing the *mappemunde,* or first map of the world that showed the New World (unlike, for example, Behaim's Nürnberg globe). The *mappemunde,* Byrd rightly points out, "represents the New World as pure potentiality, unspoiled, open space" (Byrd, 93). Looking through La Cosa's eyes Maximus performs an imaginative exercise that is essential to polis life: he sees, in Sherman Paul's words, "the New World new, for the first time; sees it as sailors in the long history of discovery saw it, emerging from the nothingness of Martin Behaim's globe" (Paul, 156).

Maximus pays respect to those Breton fishermen who had crossed the Atlantic motivated by their desire to find new fishing waters and not by greed to make a fortune out of the sea. To Maximus these first ones, or first comers, are not necessarily explorers who discover or early settlers who populate a new land. First comers are identified by their willingness not to exploit a new place but to "let it go."

> . . . the first ones
>
> on a continent which men
> have let go so our
> eyes which look
> to strike
> take nothing
> ("Capt Christopher Levett [of York]")

Davey points to the defining difference between first and second comers as being a difference between "conversion of resources into life" and "conversion of resources into money" (Davey, 311). Accordingly, Worcester and Gloucester fishermen mentioned in the Juan de la Cosa poem were all first comers: they explored and knew well the shores of Spain but did not use their knowledge to take advantage of it. Even at a

time when Europe was "being drained / of gold," they simply: "drew,
on a table, in spelt, / with a finger, in beer, a / portulans." Likewise,
the fishermen of Spain and Portugal were after fish—cod, usually, as
the name "Bacalhaos" for the New Land indicates. Because "Ships /
have always represented a large capital investment," explorers were in
the service of patron kings, feeding the royal greed to expand frontiers
so that they could usurp lands for the sake of profit. Of course, for
Maximus, such explorers as Cabot or Columbus were themselves not
driven by mercantile greed, but rather by the thirst for global knowledge. The excerpt taken from Columbus's 1498 letter still shows this
uncorrupted first-comer attitude:

> Respecting the earth, he sd,
> it is a pear, or,
> like a round ball upon a part of which there is a prominence
> like a woman's nipple, this protrusion
> is the highest & nearest to
> the sky

The fate of Columbus's disastrous fourth voyage is linked with Europe's
greed ("he lost his pearl, / he lost the Indies / to a worm"), as is the
tragedy of the *Titantic.*

In each passage of "On First Looking Out through Juan de la Cosa's
Eyes" we are given some aspect of the kind of whole world vision that
sailors and fishermen of the first-comer type have always possessed. The
mappemunde, although drafted by Juan de la Cosa, was part of the vision
of such ocean men. Their death is honored by a ritual, and so, too
4,670 Gloucester fishermen lost at sea are commemorated yearly by the
ritual of throwing flowers into the outgoing current at the Cut.

> (4,670 fishermen's lives are noticed. In an outgoing tide
> of the Annisquam River, each summer, at the August full,
> they throw flowers, which, from the current there, at the Cut,
> reach the harbor channel, and go
> these bouquets (there are few, Gloucester, who can afford florists' prices)
> float out
> > you can watch them go out into,
> the Atlantic

This same ritual is evoked in another poem of the same volume, "Maximus, to Gloucester, Sunday, July 19." As the waters of the Cut tear the

flowers off the funeral wreaths, this old polis ritual not only makes
death bearable to the living, but undoes it:

            the flowers
            turn
            the character of the sea   The sea jumps
            the fate of the flower   The drowned men are undrowned
            in the eddies
                of the eyes
                of the flowers
                opening
                the sea's eyes

            The disaster
            is undone

This whole ritual spreads "the spilling lesion / of the brillance / it is to
be alive" upon the fishing community where success, fame, and power
are of no importance: "A fisherman is not a successful man / he is not a
famous man he is not a man / of power, these are the damned by God."
However, these are men of "divine intelligence," and "What was once
received as alien," bodies and flowers, become, through this ritual, one
with the sea: "When a man's coffin is the sea / the whole of creation
shall come to his funeral."

Built into the poems that are painfully careful about facts and historical records is a more personal sequence that runs from "The Twist"
through "Letter 22." Hallberg calls it an "intermission of imaginative,
personal Letters" giving "relief from the 'COLD-SOCIAL' " (von Hallberg, 193). Dorn considers "The Twist" "the highest achievement of
The Maximus Poems," followed by "the two beautiful letters 19 and 20"
in which he praises an "attendant breathing of the first person nomina-
tive" and a "generosity" of feeling (Dorn, 306, 307). The child's vision
feeds the poetic vision here, implying, as Hallberg puts it, "that the
imaginative faculty itself—pleasant and clarifying though it is—
belongs to those who stand outside society—to poets and children"
(von Hallberg 1978, 193).

In "The Twist" Maximus reaches deep into personal memories and
dream materials to discover to the "inland waters" of the self. These
dreams appear in the poem as "trolley-cars" or "elevated railroads,"
vehicles of self-discovery in a setting of changing times and places.
Childhood memories and fantasies are woven into the dream materials,
to be explored by the sailor of "spring-tide" "inland waters." "The

nouns seem to calm themselves," notes Dorn, "and take on the
sheerings and simplicity of immediate knowledge which resides together in what is more felt, the searching substantives of the inscribed
field of Gloucester" (Dorn, 306). In a self-reflexive way, the poem is
about the writing of *The Maximus Poems* itself, reenacting the process of
archaeological excavation, whose site is the rare coincidence of self and
place. The poet discovers, again in a self-reflective way, the boyhood
discovery of a "newfoundland" inside.

> I recognize
> the country not discovera,
> the marsh behind, the ditch that Blynman made, the dog-rocks
> the tide roars over
>
> . . . .
> the whole of it
> coming,
> to this pin-point
> to turn
>
>   in this day's sun

It is "a wonderful (-filled) poem," Sherman Paul writes, "much of it
recollection and dream, [that] tells of Maximus' twisted (intertwined)
discoveries of Gloucester, sexuality, and poetry" (Paul, 157). According
to Byrd, the title refers to the fact that "the literal space in which the
poem exists is being twisted back on itself" and also to the poem's
turning back on a more subjective layer of materials (Byrd, 93). Most of
all, I think it tells of awakening adolescent sexuality ("my neap, / my
spring-tide, my / waters"), of the boy's "fantasy pleasures" and of the
change or twist it brings about.

The volume closes with "April Today Main Street," a poem expressing Maximus's sharp perceptual interchange with the phenomenal
world of Gloucester. It tells of the freshness of objects confronting the
citizen of the town, who is at home now and integral with his world:
"as poet-historian at greater ease in his place, his activities having given
it to him, enabled him to inhabit it" (Paul, 180).

Maximus Poems IV, V, VI and *The Maximus Poems: Volume Three*

After the first three sections of *Maximus* were published in 1960, this
triad form was repeated twice, resulting in the three volumes and nine

books of *The Maximus Poems* as we now have it. The second volume,
Maximus Poems IV, V, VI, was published in London in 1968 and in New
York the following year. The final volume, *The Maximus Poems: Volume
Three,* assembled by George Butterick after Olson's death, following the
poet's instructions, was published posthumously in 1975. The successive books and volumes seem to develop in a particular direction: they
become even more open in form and less linear in thematic line; historical
fact is more and more complemented by mythical and dream material;
time, space, and consciousness expand to hold a total vision of the world.
As the poem progresses, the reader's job becomes more difficult; the
poems get shorter, fragmentlike, and the reader must assume more and
more responsibility for filling in the blank spaces. More and more,
Maximus realizes the proposition Olson outlined in his essay "The Gate &
The Center": "energy is larger than man, but therefore, if he taps it as it is
in himself, his uses of himself are EXTENSIBLE in human directions &
degree not recently granted."[10] For such an immediate tapping of energies Maximus descends to the primeval origins and starts out from the
very beginning, at archetypal events and primordial awareness. *Maximus,* therefore, extends and expands in all directions, transmitting onto
his open field the abundant energy around himself.

Most Olson critics are in agreement regarding the direction and
degree of change propelling the consecutive books and volumes of
Maximus. Sherman Paul stresses Olson's new beginning that finds its
primary articulation in terms of mythical thinking (Paul, 181). Christensen contrasts the finished appearance of the first triad with the crude
and simple format of the second volume, with its draftlike, sketchy
poems that resemble a notebook or work-in-progress, its unusual and
difficult language, shifting attentions, density of allusion. In general,
Christensen regards the second triad as livelier, bolder, and more imaginative. "The single greatest effect that Olson achieves here," he points
out, "is of essence, of the pleasure of perception with a minimum of
rhetorical formality" (Christensen, 133). Don Byrd talks about rough
edges giving an unfinished quality to the poem: "the pieces seem at
times to be notes for poems rather than poetry as such," he explains;
"the minimum poetic utterance is a simple discovery, a synapse connection which establishes a necessary relationship in the on-going form"
(Byrd, 112). Merrill argues that as the poem progresses the poet's local
quest becomes a quest for inward vision, history gives way to myth,
and the whole poem becomes an "exercise in mythic magnification"
(Merrill, 195). Magnification is necessary to compensate for the reduc-

tion in man's vision that can be traced to Hellenism, according to Olson. Merrill also points to the shift in locus, from Gloucester to Dogtown, "as an obvious instance of the poet seeking a suitable arena for a cosmos of archetypes" (Merrill, 194). There is also a difference in Olson's concern (or lack of it) for interpreting his materials for the sake of better understanding. Davey characterizes these books as becoming more private and personal, for Olson no longer appends interpretive commentaries to his thematic clusters (Davey, 320). Michael Davidson sees the change more in terms of historical and spatial expansion, with Maximus as cosmic man traveling back in time and inward to psychological dimensions (Davidson, 191). Davidson finds the shift from local history to the timeless mythological present to be one of the unfortunate changes in the later books, but praises Olson for recognizing the possibilities for a more varied formal presentation.

In general, I think two qualities emerge in volumes 2 and 3 of *Maximus:* the mythic mode and the in-process design both gain more significance as the poem proceeds.

"Professionally a mythologist" (*Muthologos,* 1:61), Olson considered mythology as a "hard science" (*Muthologos,* 1:46) that granted him "the activeness, the possible activeness and personalness of experiencing," especially experiencing the earth as familiar (*Muthologos,* 1:70). For Olson, myth meant the "recognition" of "the absolute place and thing" that was his own (*Muthologos,* 1:95); myth represented a relationship, an intimate relationship that he called an "inner inherence" (Boer, 59), with the familiar. This familiar has become so much interiorized that Olson defines mythology as "the kosmos inside the human being," (*The Special View of History,* 53). This is why in these books of *Maximus* Olson's descent into prehistory and myth means also a descent into the self; for Olson, myth means "the archeology of the soul" (Paul, 182), the evolution of human spirit.[11] Such an archaeologist, especially if he is American, constantly returns to the origins, beginning again, and again. "I am beginner. I am an American." William Carlos Williams wrote.[12]

Olson's shift of interest from history to myth is expressed by the shift from Herodotus to Whitehead as spiritual influence and intellectual authority:

> & *that* concept of history (not Herodotus's,
> which was a verb, to find out for yourself:
> 'istorin, which makes any one's acts a finding out for him or her
> self, in other words restores the traum: that we act somewhere

at least by seizure, that the objective (example Thucidides, or
the latest finest tape-recorder, or any form of record on the spot

—live television or what—is a lie

as against what we know went on, the dream: the dream being
self-action with Whitehead's important corollary: that no event

is not penetrated, in intersection or collision with, an eternal
event

     The poetics of such a situation
are yet to be found out
                       ("A Later Note on Letter #15")

"The finding out" of such a poetics is traced in these volumes, following the processes by which eternal events come about. In this search for
eternal events, the poems necessarily become less biographical and
historical, and more mythic; eternal events arise out of the intersection
of an occasion and an archetype (see Paul, 183).

       . . . It is not I,
       even if the life appeared
       biographical. The only interesting thing
       is if one can be
       an image
       of man, "The nobleness, and the arete."

      (*Later:* myself (like my father, in the picture) a shadow
        on the rock.
                       ("Maximus of Gloucester")

    Christensen suggests that in the field of continuous thought that
makes up the second volume, one can distinguish categories of content,
including six subfields: the history of Gloucester, the geography and
geology of Gloucester, the origins and history of Dogtown, the marine
and fishing history of Cape Ann, the individual figures of Gloucester
and Dogtown, and myth and ancient history (Christensen, 141). But I
must note that Olson is interested in the factual-historical material only
in terms of its collision or intersection with the mythic-archetypal
histories—"An American / is a complex of occasions," he writes ("Maxi-

mus to Gloucester, Letter 27 [withheld]"). These occasions are generated by the "spiritual condition" of certain shared experiences (see
Mythologos, 2:9); of such occasions Maximus constructs "an actual earth
of value."

> an actual earth of value to
> contruct one, from rhythm to
> image, and image is knowing, and
> knowing, Confucius says, brings one
> to the goal: nothing is possible without
> doing it.
> ("*Added to / making a Republic / in gloom on
> Watchhouse / Point")

Thus, for example, Dogtown, "this / park of eternal / events," offers a
wealth of such archetypal occasions, being a rich source of eternal
events. In the Dogtown poems Maximus the mythic historian ("my
memory is / the history of time") places earth ground-center in
Dogtown, and reaches back to primordial roots of creation. In "Maximus, from Dogtown–I" Earth-Mother and Okeanos are central figures
"The sea was born of the earth") in the same way that Dogtown is the
central place in this primordial saga. Earth, sea, and rock connect with
Dogtown through the story of Andrew Merry, the bullfighter, who fell
because, having failed to acknowledge the bull's cosmic significance, he
violated sacred laws. In its dirtiness, then, Dogtown acts as a microcosm for the nation:

> . . . the Harbor
>
> the shore the City
> are now
> shitty, as the Nation
>
> is . . .
> ("Maximus, from Dogtown–II")

Not only is Dogtown "Carbon" in a negative way, but it also contains
those archetypes that activate the universe—"The earth with a city in
her hair / entangled of trees" (3:289). Thus, as "the dog town / of the
mother city," it is the polis of various maternal and paternal archetypes,
as well as archetypes of the earth reminding us of its animate nature

through its storms, volcanos, and geysers (see "Letter #41 [broken off].") Maximus reaches back to these archetypes, because he is driven by a desire to reconstitute this sense of being alive.

> that forever the geography
> which leans in
> on me I compel
> backwards I compel Gloucester
> to yield, to
> change
>   Polis
> is this
> ("Maximus to Gloucester, Letter 27 [withheld]")

Poems are arranged chronologically throughout these sections, too, as the search for individuation and for the sacred and eternal events continues in a spiral motion. The text is loaded with mythological and cosmic references, with recurring motifs borrowed from ancient stories, legends, ballads, and chronicles; these motifs provide Olson with material to weave a visionary poetry of synthesis rather than teaching. Hallberg sees the convention of assertion working in these later books, where "the mythological narrative self-consciously posits the poet's right to appropriate perspective. . . . Maximus is more the seer than the teacher" (von Hallberg 1978, 134–35).

As Maximus's attention is captured by eternal events and objects in their rawness and concentration, his narrative becomes more and more discontinuous and fragmented. The poems become shorter, notelike sketches, without any possibility for discursive order. Rhythm and image become the primary units for construction: "There is no strict personal order / for my inheritance" ("Maximus to Gloucester, Letter 27 [withheld]").

Maximus's projective field is constructed out of direct and immediate responses to phenomena. Byrd calls this sense of form *postrational:* "the *field* of the poem includes not only the data which can be comprehended by humanistic rationalism but also all that humanistic rationalism excludes as irrational, random, or subjective" (Byrd, 45). This is very important, I think, because readers can only apprehend *Maximus,* especially the later books, and derive pleasure from it, if they adopt an approach that goes counter to all traditional approaches. The reader must unlearn conventional reading strategies, and take a stance of obedience and openness. The poem's success lies with the trust the reader grants it and with the reader's negative capability. Failure to comprehend poems can be frustrating, but the overall sense one gets from the book as a whole—often encouraged on the way by glimpses of revelation and enlightenment—more than compensates for specific obscurities. Such reading shall grant us the privileged sense of being part of the whole, having participated, through the discrete experiences of the individual poems, in that restoration of wholeness that Maximus attempted with a heightened awareness of the polis-kosmos "inside the human being." In the final perception of synthesis, we become integral parts of *apophaines-thai,* that harmony "which shows forth."

> Paradise is a person. Come into this world.
> The soul is a magnificent Angel.
>
> . . . .
>
> apophainesthai
> got hidden all the years
> apophainesthai: the soul,
> in its progressive rise
>
> apophainesthai
> passes in & out
> of more difficult things
> and by so passing
> apophainesthai
> the act which actuates the soul itself—
>
> . . . .
>
> apophainesthai
> its ascent is its own mirage
>
>   ("Maximus, at the Harbor")

Conclusion

Charles Olson is arguably the most complex and far-ranging American poet of the past 50 years, but the meaning of his work is still, to a considerable degree, an unexplored continent. A man of vast reading and daring intellect, his poetry is often difficult to follow, not because of vagueness—Olson is never vague—but because his writings are overloaded with material, demanding great intellectual effort on the part of the reader.

Radicalism is perhaps the word that first comes to one's mind when trying to give an assessment of his achievement—radicalism in writing, thinking, politics, and life-style dictated by a passion and greed for imaginative and intellectual alternatives. Giving an estimate of Olson's radicalism, Paul Christensen also sees Olson as overtowering; he suggests that "The so-called radical politics of the 1960s were second rate compared to the vision expressed by Charles Olson a decade earlier. Olson was, quite simply, the purest instance of the radical imagination of the midcentury. . . . With Olson at its center, . . . the 'drab Fifties' were a time of luminous new perceptions and of innovations whose strengths have not played out some forty years later."[1] With his ideas on *humilitas* and ecology, Christian orthodoxy, the native roots of American culture, the rejection of the "humanism" and "ego-position" of Western civilization, he predicted the breakup of the monolithic Anglo-American sensibility into a diverse, multiracial consciousness. Translated into demonstration slogans, these ideas turned into social equality, Black power, and women's liberation.

Yet for a long time Olson remained the target of ridicule. His philosophic, scientific, and aesthetic radicalism was alien to mainstream American writing. The most common charge leveled against him (by James Dickey, for example) stated that he was derivative, especially of Pound. Olson scholarship, however, has steadily emerged to refute such claims. *Olson* is a journal solely devoted to this scholarship; *boundary 2* published an Olson issue in 1973. Topics such as his life, his affinities to his masters (Melville, Lawrence, Pound, Williams), and his place in Black Mountain College have been explored by such critics as Ann Charters, Catherine Seelye, Charles Boer, Fielding

Dawson, and Martin Duberman. His significant correspondence with
Creeley is being published, and his correspondence with Dahlberg and
Joyce Benson have also been published. The University of Connecticut
maintains his archives at Storrs, and the *Maximus Poems* and his *Collected
Poems* have been issued in definitive editions. Eminent scholars, including George F. Butterick, Sherman Paul, Charles Altieri, Joseph
Riddell, Rober von Hallberg, William Spanos, Paul Bové, Michael
Davidson, Egbert Faas, and Paul Christensen, have written extensively
on Olson. William McPherson has brought out a complete bibliography of Olson and related writings. Twenty years after his death, today
he indeed occupies, in Robert Duncan's words, "an area in history big
enough for some spirit size" (quoted in *Muthologos,* 2:97).

Notes and References

Preface

1. "A Bibliography on America for Ed Dorn," in *Additional Prose,* ed. George F. Butterick (Bolinas, Calif.: Four Seasons Foundation, 1974), 11.

Chapter One

1. *Muthologos. The Collected Interviews and Lectures,* 2 vols., ed. George F. Butterick (Bolinas, Calif.: Four Seasons Foundation, vol. 1., 1978; vol. 2, 1979), 1:111; hereafter cited in the text.

2. *Charles Olson and Robert Creeley: The Complete Correspondence,* ed. George F. Butterick (Santa Barbara, Calif.: Black Sparrow Press, 1980), 1:19; hereafter cited in the text as *Olson-Creeley Correspondence.*

3. Charles Boer, *Charles Olson in Connecticut* (Chicago: Swallow Press, 1975), 38; hereafter cited in the text.

4. Martin Duberman, *Black Mountain: An Exploration in Community* (New York: E. P. Dutton & Co., 1972), 382; hereafter cited in the text.

5. "The Letters of Edward Dahlberg and Charles Olson," ed. Paul Christensen, *Sulfur* 2 (1981): 131.

6. Joel Oppenheimer, quoted in Duberman, *Black Mountain,* 378.

7. Robert Duncan, quoted in Ann Charters, *Olson/Melville: A Study in Affinity* (Berkeley: Oyez, 1968), 17; hereafter cited in the text.

8. William Moebius, " 'Spiritus ubi vult spirat': On Charles Olson," *boundary 2* 11, nos. 1–2 (Fall 1973–Winter 1974):16.

9. Jonathan Williams, quoted in Duberman, *Black Mountain,* 384.

10. Fielding Dawson, "On Olson, with References to Guy Davenport," *Sagetrieb* 1, no. 1 (Spring 1982): 126; hereafter cited in the text.

11. Ed Dorn, quoted in William McPheron, *Charles Olson: The Critical Reception, 1941–1983. A Bibliographic Guide* (New York: Garland Publishing, 1986), xvi.

12. Quoted in "Introduction," *Charles Olson & Ezra Pound: An Encounter at St. Elizabeths,* ed. Catherine Seelye (New York: Grossman Publishers, 1975), xxiii; hereafter cited in the text.

13. *The Post Office: A Memoir of His Father* (Bolinas, Calif.: Grey Fox Press, 1975), 43; hereafter cited in the text as *Post Office.*

14. Olson's inscription in Dahlberg's copy of *Call Me Ishmael,* as quoted in John Cech, *Charles Olson and Edward Dahlberg: A Portrait of a Friendship* (University of Victoria, British Columbia: English Literary Studies, Monograph Series, no. 27, 1982), 90; hereafter cited in the text.

15. "The Letters of Edward Dahlberg and Charles Olson. Introduction: Part One. The Early Years (1936–1948)," ed. Paul Christensen, *Sulfur* 1 (1981): 107, 108.

16. Ted Dreier describing the college to Josef Albers in 1933; quoted in Duberman, *Black Mountain,* 56; hereafter cited in the text as Duberman.

17. Michael Rumaker, "Robert Creeley at Black Mountain," *boundary 2* 6, no:3–7, no. 1 (Spring–Fall 1978): 140.

18. "Introductory Statement for Black Mountain College Catalog, Spring Semester, 1952," *Olson* 2 (Fall 1974): 25–26; quoted in Merrill, 16.

19. Robert Duncan in a taped interview with Ann Charters; quoted in *The Special View of History,* ed. Ann Charters (Berkeley, Calif.: Oyez, 1970), 11.

20. John Cech, "Olson Teaching," *Maps* 4 (1971): 72; quoted by William Aiken in "Charles Olson and the Vatic," *boundary 2* 11, nos. 1–2 (Fall 1973–Winter 1974): 26.

21. Robert Creeley, tape interview, quoted by Ann Charters in "Introduction," *Special View of History,* 2.

22. William Aiken, "Charles Olson and the Vatic," 33–34.

Chapter Two

1. "Projective Verse," in *Selected Writings of Charles Olson,* ed. Robert Creeley (New York: New Directions, 1966), 6; hereafter cited in the text as "PV."

2. Robert Creeley, "Introduction" to *Selected Writings,* 7.

3. William Carlos Williams, "The Poem as a Field of Action" [1948], in *Selected Essays* (New York: New Directions, 1969), 283, 290.

4. Thomas F. Merrill, *The Poetry of Charles Olson: A Primer* (Newark: University of Delaware Press, 1982), 48–49; hereafter cited in the text.

5. Paul Christensen, *Charles Olson: Call Him Ishmael* (Austin: University of Texas Press, 1979), 71; hereafter cited in the text.

6. Charles Altieri, "Placing Creeley's Recent Work: A Poetics of Conjecture," *boundary 2* 6, no. 3, 7, no. 1 (Spring–Fall 1978); 176; hereafter cited in the text.

7. Denise Levertov, "Some Notes on Organic Form," in *The Poet in the World* (New York: New Directions, 1973), 13.

8. Ekbert Faas, "Charles Olson," in *Towards a New American Poetics: Essays and Interviews* (Santa Barbara, Calif.: Black Sparrow Press, 1978), 47; hereafter cited in the text.

9. Quoted in Robert Creeley, "Introduction to Charles Olson II," in *A Quick Graph: Collected Notes and Essays,* ed. Donald Allen (San Francisco: Four Seasons Foundation, 1970), 185.

10. Charles Altieri, *Self and Sensibility in Contemporary American Poetry*

(Cambridge: Cambridge University Press, 1984), 91; hereafter cited in the text.

11. Robert Creeley, *Contexts of Poetry,* ed. Donald Allen (Bolinas, Calif.: Four Seasons Foundation, 1973), 34–35; hereafter cited in the text.

12. Robert Creeley, "Olson & Others: Some Orts for the Sports," in *A Quick Graph,* 163.

13. Robert Creeley, "Charles Olson: *Y & X,*" in *A Quick Graph,* 151; hereafter cited in the text by title.

14. Alan Golding, "Olson's Metrical Thicket: Toward a Theory of Free Verse Prosody," *Language and Style,* 14, no. 1 (Winter 1981): 64, hereafter cited in the text.

15. "Human Universe," in *Human Universe and Other Essays,* ed. Donald Allen (San Francisco: Averhahn Society, 1965), 53; hereafter cited in the text as "HU."

16. Robert Creeley, "Some Notes on Olson's Maximus," in *A Quick Graph,* 172.

17. Robert von Hallberg, "Olson, Whitehead, and the Objectivists," *boundary 2* 11, nos. 1–2 (Fall 1973–Winter 1974): 87; hereafter cited in the text as von Hallberg 1974.

Chapter Three

1. János Bolyai, *Appendix. The Theory of Space,* ed. Ferenc Kárteszi (Budapest: Akadémiai Kiadó, 1987), 26.

2. Werner Heisenberg, *Physics and Philosophy: The Revolution in Modern Science* (London: Allen & Unwin, 1958), 123.

3. Alfred North Whitehead, *Science and the Modern World* (Cambridge: Cambridge University Press, 1953), 110.

4. D. H. Lawrence, "Making Pictures," in *Selected Essays* (Hammondsworth, England: Penguin, 1950), 303; hereafter cited in the text.

5. *Letters for Origin, 1950–1956,* ed. Albert Glover (London: Cape Goliard Press/Grossman Publishers, 1970), 10, 11; hereafter cited in the text as *LO.*

6. Werner Heisenberg, *Philosophic Problems of Nuclear Science,* trans. F. C. Hayes (London: Faber, 1962), 11.

7. Quoted in Bolyai, *Appendix,* 30.

8. See George F. Butterick, "Editing Postmodern Texts," *Sulfur* 11 (1984): 117; hereafter cited in the text as Butterick 1984.

9. Charles Stein, "Olson and Jung: The Projection of Archetypal Force onto Language," *New Wilderness Letter* 11, no. 8 (Spring 1980): 50; hereafter cited in the text.

10. Robert Kern, "Composition as Recognition: Robert Creeley and Postmodern Poetics," *boundary 2* 6, no. 3–7, no. 1 (Spring–Fall 1978): 218.

11. "Letter to Vincent Ferrini," in *The Gist of Origin*, ed. Cid Corman (New York: Grossman Publishers, 1975), 4.

12. Stephen Fredman, *Poet's Prose: The Crisis in American Verse* (Cambridge: Cambridge University Press, 1983), 30; hereafter cited in the text.

13. Hugh Kenner, *A Homemade World: The American Modernist Writers* (New York: William Morrow, 1975), 60.

14. William Moebius, "*Spiritus ubi vult spirat:* On Charles Olson," *boundary 2* 11, nos. 1–2 (Fall 1973–Winter 1974): 18.

15. John Keats, letter to George and Thomas Keats (21 Dec. 1817), in *Selected Letters*, ed. Robert Pack (New York: Signet, 1974), 55.

16. I. A. Richards, "Rhythm and Metre," in *The Structure of Verse*, ed. Harvey Gross (New York: Ecco Press, 1979), 68, 75.

Chapter Four

1. Sherman Paul, *Olson's Push: Origin, Black Mountain, and Recent American Poetry* (Baton Rouge: Louisiana State University Press, 1978), 4; hereafter cited in the text.

2. William Aiken, *boundary 2*, 29.

3. Robert von Hallberg, *Charles Olson: The Scholar's Art* (Cambridge: Harvard University Press, 1978), 7; hereafter cited in the text as von Hallberg 1978.

4. Guy Davenport, "Scholia and Conjectures for Olson's 'the Kingfishers,' " *boundary 2* 11, nos. 1–2 (Fall 1973–Winter 1974): 250.

5. Thomas Merrill, 84, quoting Olson, "Memorial Letter," *Origin*, no. 20 (January 1971): 47.

6. Burton Hatten, "Kinesis and hearing: 'The Kingfishers' and the Critics,' " *sagetrieb* (forthcoming).

7. The intrepretations Hatlen refers to are: Sherman Paul, *Olson's Push;* Robert von Hallberg, *Charles Olson;* Carol Kyle, "The Mesoamerican Cultural Past and Charles Olson's 'The Kingfishers,' " *Alcheringa/Ethnopoetics* 1 (1975): 68–77; Guy Davenport, "Scholia and Conjectures for Olson's 'The Kingfishers' "; Thomas F. Merrill, *The Poetry of Charles Olson;* Maxine Combs, "Charles Olson's 'The Kingfishers,': A Consideration of Meaning and Method," *Far Point* 4 (1970): 66–76; Paul Christensen, *Charles Olson.*

8. The first is Guy Davenport's translation (see Fielding Dawson, "On Olson, with References to Guy Davenport," 126), while the second is Sherman Paul's (Paul, 11).

9. See Hallberg's interpretation in *Charles Olson*, 91 ff.

10. "The E at Delphi," *Plutarch's Moralia*, trans. Frank Cole Babbitt, (Cambridge: Harvard University Press, Loeb Classical Library, 1936), 5:391. As quoted by von Hallberg, *Charles Olson*, 24.

11. Robert Creeley, "Some Notes on Olson's *Maximus*," in *A Quick Graph*, 168–69.

12. Robert Creeley, "A Quick Glance," in *A Quick Graph,* 155.

13. Robert J. Bertholf, "Righting the Balance: *The Distances,*" *boundary 2* 2, nos. 1–2 (Fall 1973–Winter 1974): 230; hereafter cited in the text.

14. Ezra Pound, *ABC of Reading* (London: Faber, 1951), 34.

15. Charles Altieri, *Enlarging the Temple: New Directions in American Poetry during the 1960s* (Lewisburg, Pa.: Bucknell University Press, 1979), 103; hereafter cited in the text.

Chapter Five

1. Michael Davidson, "Charles Olson, *The Maximus Poems,* ed. George Butterick," *Sulfur* 9 (1984): 188; hereafter cited in the text.

2. George F. Butterick, "Introduction" to *A Guide to "The Maximus Poems" of Charles Olson* (Berkeley and Los Angeles: University of California Press, 1978), xxi; hereafter cited in the text as Butterick 1978.

3. Clayton Eshleman, "Charles Olson's Death and the Fate of the Self," manuscript draft; hereafter cited in the text as Eshleman MS.

4. Robert Duncan in a tape-recorded lecture from 1961, quoted in Frank Davey, "Six Readings of Olson's *Maximus,*" *boundary 2* 11, nos. 1–2 (Fall 1973–Winter 1974): 300; hereafter cited in the text.

5. Don Byrd, *Charles Olson's "Maximus"* (Urbana: University of Illinois Press, 1980), 64; hereafter cited in the text.

6. Robert Duncan, "Notes on Poetics Regarding Olson's *Maximus,*" in *The Poetics of the New American Poetry,* ed. Donald M. Allen and Warren Tallman (New York: Grove Press, 1973), 188; hereafter cited in the text.

7. Robert Creeley, "Some Notes on Olson's *Maximus,*" 169.

8. Ed Dorn, "What I See in *The Maximus Poems,*" in *The Poetics of the New American Poetry,* ed. Donald M. Allen and Warren Tallman (New York: Grove Press, 1973), 296, 299.

9. L. S. Dembo, "Olson's *Maximus* and the Way to Knowledge," *boundary 2* 11, nos. 1–2 (Fall 1973–Winter 1974): 288; hereafter cited in the text.

10. "The Gate and the Center," in *Human Universe,* 22.

11. See Robert Duncan, "The Truth and Life of Myth," in *Fictive Certainties* (New York: New Directions, 1985).

12. William Carlos Williams, *Imaginations* (1938; New York: New Directions, 1970), 175.

Conclusion

1. Paul Christensen, "The Achievement of George Butterick," *Sulfur* 21 (Winter 1988): 4.

Selected Bibliography

Primary Works

Collected Volumes

The Collected Poems of Charles Olson. Edited by George F. Butterick. Berkeley and Los Angeles: University of California Press, 1987.

The Maximus Poems, edited by George F. Butterick. Berkeley and Los Angeles: University of California Press, 1983.

Books of Poetry

Archaeologist of Morning. London: Cape Goliard, 1970.

The Distances. New York: Grove Press; London: Evergreen Books, 1960.

In Cold Hell, in Thicket. Dorchester, Mass.: Origin, 1953. Issued as *Origin* 8 (Winter 1953).

Maximus, From Dogtown-1. San Francisco: Auerhahn, 1961.

The Maximus Poems, 1-10. Stuttgart, Germany: Jonathan Williams, 1953.

Maximus Poems, 11-22. Stuttgart, Germany: Jonathan Williams, 1956.

The Maximus Poems. New York: Jargon/Corinth Books, 1960.

Maximus Poems IV, V, VI. London: Cape Goliard Press; New York: Grossman Publishers, 1968.

The Maximus Poems: Volume Three. Edited by Charles Boer and George F. Butterick. New York: Grossman Publishers, 1975.

O'Ryan. San Fransisco: White Rabbit Press, 1965.

Some Early Poems. Iowa City: Windhover Press, University of Iowa, 1978.

Y & X. Washington, D.C.: Black Sun Press, 1948.

Fiction

The Fiery Hunt and Other Plays. Bolinas, Calif.: Four Seasons Foundation, 1977.

The Post Office: A Memoir of His Father. Bolinas, Calif.: Grey Fox Press, 1975. Short Stories.

Nonfiction

Additional Prose: A Bibliography on America, Proprioception & Other Notes & Essays. Edited by George F. Butterick. Bolinas, Calif.: Four Seasons Foundation, 1974.

A Bibliography on America for Ed Dorn. San Francisco: Four Seasons Foundation, 1964.

Call Me Ishmael. New York: Reynal & Hitchcock, 1947.

Causal Mythology. San Francisco: Four Seasons Foundation, 1969.

Charles Olson & Ezra Pound: An Encounter at St. Elizabeths. Edited by Catherine Seelye. New York: Grossman Publishers, 1975.

Human Universe and Other Essays. Edited by Donald Allen. San Francisco: Auerhahn Society, 1965.

"Lear and Moby-Dick." *Twice-a-Year* (Fall–Winter 1938): 165–89. *Muthologos: Collected Interviews and Lectures.* 2 vols. Edited by George F. Butterick. Bolinas, Calif.: Four Seasons Foundation, 1978–79.

Poetry and Truth: The Beloit Lectures and Poems. Edited by George F. Butterick. San Francisco: Four Seasons Foundation, 1971.

"Projective Verse." *Poetry New York* 3 (1950): 13–22.

Proprioception. San Francisco: Four Seasons Foundation, 1965.

Reading at Berkeley. Bolinas, Calif.: Coyote, 1966.

Selected Writings of Charles Olson. Edited by Robert Creeley. New York: New Directions, 1966.

The Special View of History. Edited by Ann Charters. Berkeley, Calif.: Oyez, 1970.

Correspondence

Charles Olson and Robert Creeley: The Complete Correspondence. Edited by George F. Butterick. Santa Barbara, Calif.: Black Sparrow Press, 1980– [in progress].

Letters for Origin, 1950–1956. Edited by Albert Glover. London: Cape Goliard Press / Grossman Publishers, 1970.

"The Letters of Edward Dahlberg and Charles Olson." Edited by Paul Christensen. *Sulfur* 1 (1981): 104–68; 2 (1981): 65–166; 3 (1982): 122–223.

"Letters to Vincent Ferrini." In *The Gist of Origin,* edited by Cid Corman, 3–4. New York: Grossman Publishers, 1975.

Mayan Letters. Edited by Robert Creeley. Palma de Mallorca: Divers Press, 1953.

"Memorial Letter." *Origin,* no. 20 (January 1971): 46–48.

Pleistocene Man: Letters from Charles Olson to John Clarke during October 1965. Buffalo, N.Y.: Institute of Further Studies, 1968.

Secondary Works

Altieri, Charles. *Enlarging the Temple: New Directions in American Poetry during the 1960s.* Lewisburg, Pa.: Bucknell University Press, 1979. An influential book on the American poets of the sixties, treating them as inheritors of symbolist and immanentist modes; Olson is placed among such poets of the immanentist experience as Bly and O'Hara.

Boer, Charles. *Charles Olson in Connecticut*. Chicago: Swallow Press, 1975. A moving personal account of the last six months of Olson's life, told by the poet's friend and companion.

Charters, Ann. *Olson/Melville: A Study in Affinity*. Berkeley, Calif.: Oyez, 1968. An important study of the Olson-Melville affinity, the concept of projective space that Olson learned from *Moby-Dick,* and Olson's involvement in the uniqueness of the American experience.

Christensen, Paul. *Charles Olson: Call Him Ishmael*. Austin: University of Texas Press, 1979. One of the most important introductions to Olson's work, focusing on a wide range of topics from projectivism to *The Maximus Poems,* as well as on Olson's ties with the Black Mountain generation of poets.

Duberman, Martin. *Black Mountain: An Exploration in Community*. New York: E. P. Dutton & Co., 1972. A classic account of the ideas, persons, and goings-on that made Black Mountain College.

Faas, Ekbert. "Charles Olson." In *Towards a New American Poetics,* edited by Ekbert Faas, 39–51. Santa Barbara, Calif.: Black Sparrow Press, 1978. A definitive study placing Olson in the tradition of Pound, Zukofsky, and Williams, mostly stressing Lawrence's importance for Olson's poetics.

McPheron, William. *Charles Olson: The Critical Reception, 1941–1983. A Bibliographic Guide*. New York and London: Garland Publishing, 1986. A long-awaited bibliography of Olson scholarship.

Merrill, Thomas F. *The Poetry of Charles Olson: A Primer*. Newark: University of Delaware Press, 1982. A very readable account of Olson's achievement as a poet and thinker; discusses in detail the "Grammar of Illiteracy" that illuminates his philosophic stand. Deals mostly with the shorter poems, but touches upon *Maximus,* too.

Paul, Sherman. *Olson's Push: Origin, Black Mountain, and Recent American Poetry*. Baton Rouge: Louisiana State University Press, 1978. Discusses Olson's grand achievement as poet and essayist, his reconsideration of history and cosmos, tradition and mythology, place and *polis*.

von Hallberg, Robert. "Olson, Whitehead, and the Objectivists." *boundary 2* 11, nos. 1–2 (Fall 1973–Winter 1974):85–111. A powerful study of Olson's affinity to Whitehead's concept of order as process as an alternative to the humanistic concept of man as order.

von Hallberg, Robert. *Charles Olson. The Scholar's Art*. Cambridge: Harvard University Press, 1978. An erudite introduction to Olson's philosophy, illustrated by advanced interpretations of individual poems.

Index

The Author

Associate professor of American studies in Szeged and Budapest, Hungary, Enikő Bollobás completed her studies in Budapest, Minneapolis, and La Jolla, California. She was Fulbright visiting professor at the University of Oregon in Eugene and is the author of *Tradition and Innovation in American Free Verse: Whitman to Duncan* (1986). Bollobás has been active in the Hungarian political opposition since the early 1980s and is especially interested in human rights under totalitarianism. In 1988 she became the founding member of the Hungarian Democratic Forum, the largest opposition party to emerge during the revolutionary changes of 1988–89 and has since worked as the Forum's foreign affairs spokesperson, lecturing internationally. In 1990 she was appointed Minister counselor and deputy chief of mission of the Embassy of Hungary in Washington, D.C.

The Editor

Warren French (Ph.D., University of Texas, Austin) retired from Indiana University in 1986 and is now an honorary professor associated with the Board of American Studies at the University College of Swansea, Wales. In 1985 Ohio University awarded him a doctor of humane letters. He has contributed volumes to Twayne's United States Authors Series on Jack Kerouac, Frank Norris, John Steinbeck, and J. D. Salinger. His most recent publication for Twayne is *The San Francisco Poetry Renaissance, 1955–1960.*